PULSE

You Can't Heal
What You Can't Feel

ROB LINK

2011 Reformed Church Press

Dedication

This book is dedicated to Kristy, who lived through years of my issues. You endured with patience, loved well, prayed me to freedom, helped me become who I am today, and made life much better. Thank you. I love you. I think you're special. And I'm glad to be your husband.

Thanks!

Thanks Kristy, for being passionate about your times with the Lord long before I was. Thank you for being the best wife I could ever imagine having. Your support, encouragement, laughter, and love have simply made my life.

Thanks Jake, Max, Zeke, Reese, and Elyse for adding so much to my life. Being your dad is the second best thing in the world (just behind being your mom's husband). I love you guys a ton.

Thanks Barkly for being a cool dog. You are a wonderful greeter at church. I'm glad you get to come to work with me every day.

Thanks Mom. None of this would have happened without you. You introduced me to Jesus. You've loved me well. You are a great mom, a great mom-in-law, and a phenomenal grandma. I'm glad you are my mom and my friend.

Thanks River Church for your support, care, fruit, and passion for people of all kinds. Thank you for embracing the vision that the Lord was gracious enough to give to a knucklehead like me. You've made what I dreamed a church could be a reality.

Thank you both current and past River elders for encouragement, love, tangible appreciation, support, and oversight. Wouldn't want to lead a church without you all.

Thanks River staff: Wil, Fraaz, Doreen, Rod, Anna, Judy, Susan. You are awesome. How many people get to work side by side with people as remarkable as you all? Staff meetings are always a highlight of my week.

Band of Couples (you know who you are). You make Kristy's and my marriage better. Thanks for the sharpening, listening, fun, and loving.

Wil and Fraaz. You guys are crazy. Crazy awesome that is. I regularly thank God for you both. I am so thankful that I get to work every day with two of my best friends. You guys have been with me as I struggled with stuff. You've challenged me to be freer. You've picked me up when I was down. You've made Jesus' words about abundant life (John 10:10) a reality for me. Thanks for pushing me to put my butt in the chair to write.

Little bird, uh...I mean Vink, I love working with you in the multiplication movement. Thanks for leading me. Thanks for making this book happen. You've been an agent of the Lord to further the fruit he had in store for me to bear. You did cheat at *Dance Revolution* though.

Ann and Barb. You are the dynamic duo of the publishing and editing world. Your work is fantastic. Your insights right on. Your excitement infectious. Your encouragement life giving. I don't think I would have kept writing without you two. Thank you.

Pulse
You Can't Heal What You Can't Feel

Part 1: If You Have a Pulse You Have Issues

Chapter 1
Fine

It was very clear. Plain as the nose on my face. Not a single person at church had any issues whatsoever. Except, of course, me. Church was filled with people who were entirely without anything negative in their lives.

How did I know this, you might ask? It was obvious. When I was a kid, "How are you?" was a question I heard people at church ask each other every Sunday morning. And every single time I overheard the response it was something along the lines of, "Fine. How are you?" Not once did I hear someone say, "Today has been a rough day" or "I got in a fight with my brother" or "I'm sad." Everyone was fine. Everyone, that is, except one person—me. I knew deep inside that I wasn't always fine. There were days in my life that were rough. Sometimes I did fight with my brother. And some days I was just plain old sad.

Something else was clear: I was messed up in a world where no one else was. I was sad when no one else seemed to be. I had struggles when no one else did. I had issues. No one else did. There was something wrong with me. Everyone else was always fine. I was only fine some of the time. Something was definitely wrong with me. This was a tough pill to swallow for an elementary-school-age kid. I tried to deny it. Yet the more I looked around, the more it sunk in. I had issues and no one else did.

Maybe you've felt the same way. Have you ever, when asked how your day was going, told someone you were having a bad day? Have you ever been honest and said, "Today just stinks"? Try it sometime, and watch the reaction you get. You might get stared at as if you had three noses. The inquirer might stutter, "Well...ah...um...I...ah..." then turn and run like a bat out of Hades.

Like others who have encountered such reactions, I realized back in my youth that I had just one option. I, too, needed to appear "fine" whatever the cost.

So I learned to play the game. And I played it well. I looked like the epitome of fine. When I felt bad, I never let it show. Big boys don't cry, and I wanted to be a big boy. "Never show your weakness" was my battle cry. "Suck it up" became my mantra. I became the king of fine. Failed a test?—no problem, I was fine. Rejected by peers?—no problem, I was fine. In trouble at home?—no problem, I was fine. Fine, fine, fine. I was just fine. Always fine.

The problem was that I wasn't always fine. My head said "fine," but my heart said "not fine." Over the years, as I listened to my head, my heart slowly died. Without knowing it, I became a walking dead man. Or as the Old Testament prophet Ezekiel says, I had a heart of stone. Cold. Hard. Unfeeling. Dead. This was not good.

Not allowing myself to feel bad eventually led to my not being able to feel good either. It was as if the Novocain I used to numb icky feelings seeped into the good feelings. I became blah. I tried to combat this by running after things that I thought would bring me back to life. We all have a deep-down craving to experience life—to live an abundant life. My heart of stone led me to run after things that seemed like they would satisfy my craving to feel alive. Pornography. For a moment I felt alive. But only for a moment. Escape through novels. For a time I felt free. But only for a time. Food. Bunches of food. For a time I felt fantastic. But only for a time, and then I felt sick. Drink. Gallons of Mountain Dew. I couldn't go more than a couple of hours without it. For a few hours I felt invigorated. But only for a few hours. Eventually I began to shut down. I couldn't hide from the nagging thought that still lurked in the back of my mind. I was not fine.

The breaking began one afternoon when my friend Jaime asked me, "How are you?" Of course I answered, "Fine, I'm fine." I wanted to get out of the spotlight as soon as I could, so I quickly asked, "How are you?" But Jaime didn't play by the rules. He didn't answer my question. Instead he said, "Really? Your parents' divorce was finalized yesterday. They called it quits after twenty-six years of marriage. How can you be fine?"

Can you believe it? What a goofball, I thought. He's not supposed to do that. I went into cover-my-backside mode. "Oh, I'm fine, really fine. I...ah...gotta go. Bye." Walking away, I broke out in a cold sweat. That was close. My un-fineness had nearly been uncovered. And that couldn't happen. I was the only one I knew who had issues, and I had to hide them at all costs. After all, everyone else was fine.

But by this time, other thoughts were creeping in.

For starters, if everyone was fine, why in the world did Jesus say he had come "to heal the brokenhearted"? (Luke 4:18, KJV). Apparently in my church there were no brokenhearted people. But if everyone really had it all together, why did Jesus say, "[I]n this life you will have trouble"? (John 16:33). People didn't seem to have trouble in the world I observed around me. Yet, if everything was hunky dory, why did James say, "Consider it pure joy...whenever you face trials of many kinds"? (James 1:2). The folks around me didn't seem to need James's pep talk.

As the years passed, more and more I found comfort in the passages in the Bible about trials and trouble and being brokenhearted. I began to think maybe I wasn't the only person with issues. Maybe God had put such things in the Bible to encourage people like me who had issues. I had hope that maybe, just maybe, having a stinky day was a normal part of life.

As I pondered these thoughts, the still, small voice of the Lord whispered something life-changing to me. The Spirit of God spoke to my heart: "If you have a pulse, you have issues." At first I thought I had heard wrong. My experience within the community of Christian believers had taught me a different reality. Yet the gentle voice of the Lord continued to repeat: "If you have a pulse, you have issues."

I continued to wrestle with this revelation. "God," I said, "if that's true, then every living person has issues." "Exactly," is the response I heard within. Exactly. If you have a pulse, you have issues. As I read my Bible I couldn't believe I had missed this simple truth. It was all over the Scriptures. Even the people chosen by God to do great things had issues! Abraham was a scaredy cat who didn't trust God to protect him so he told a king that his wife was his sister—twice! Moses was chicken and made all kinds of excuses because he didn't want to do what God asked him to do. When God called Gideon to fight for Israel, Gideon was found cowering in a winepress, hiding from Israel's enemies.

My goodness, I thought, there's a theme here: Bible people being scared! David lusted, committed adultery, and murdered. Samson had woman issues. The apostle Peter was always putting his foot in his mouth. Paul (when he was Saul) was mean and killed every Christian he could find. Paul and Barnabas had a nasty split.

And when it came to being brokenhearted, even Jesus had issues. When his buddy Lazarus died he didn't put a "stiff upper lip" on it; he wept. The night he was betrayed, Jesus clearly was not fine. In deep anguish he sweated drops of blood.

How in the world had I missed it?! If you have a pulse, you have issues.

Taking in this revelation was like breathing fresh air. Ahhhh, I'm not abnormal. I'm not the only person in the world who isn't fine. Not only that—I was in good company. I remember the power of this revelation speaking to my heart: to be human is to hurt. Not all the time, but sometimes. In fact, I realized, a life devoid of pain is really no life at all. We were made to feel joy, to be sure. Yet what is joy without sorrow? What is happy without sad? What is laughter without crying? To be fully alive includes having a bad day from time to time. Maybe a better way to say this is: to be fully alive includes feeling bad as the bad comes our way.

This new thinking led me to new freedom. Freedom to feel bad. Freedom to feel. I didn't care if I was the only who seemed to have issues. Life is more than what it seems. I was so tired of feeling like I had to pretend all was well. For the first time I could remember in my adult life, I allowed myself to feel.

And that's when depression reared its ugly head.

Allowing myself to feel bad opened a floodgate of emotions that I had pent-up deep inside. Once the gate was open, I couldn't shut it. Pain just kept flowing out, and then depression flowed in. I felt totally unprepared to deal with my negative emotions.

Looking back, I can see that I had been depressed, to varying degrees, for a number of years. Two ulcers in high school had been chalked up to poor eating habits. Moodiness had been written off as being caused by a lack of sleep. My withdrawal from people was explained away with the word introvert. Now I can see that these were all signs that I was wrestling with depression.

As I came to grips with depression, I sought the help of a gifted, godly counselor—one of the best decisions I have ever made. I quickly learned that feeling bad was not the cause of depression. Not feeling bad was what caused it. In other words, not dealing with pain was at the root of my deep-seated funk. Ignoring the yuckiness only gave the yuckiness power to haunt my life. My therapist said that I needed to find the source of the pain and deal with it. Frankly that sounded about as fun as sitting on a cactus wearing a Speedo.

It was obvious right away that I had no idea where my pain came from. After all, my parents were cool. I was never abused. I was received well in school. I had heard stories of people who had all kinds of horrific things happen to them. The source of their pain was obvious. The source of mine?—not so obvious. I had trained myself so well to ignore the issues in my life that I no longer could identify them. How in the world was I going to discover the root of the junk? And then how was I going to deal with it?

Parts two and three of this book answer those two questions. Part two lays out the process that I walked through (with the help of my therapist) to discover the source of my issues and then to get free from the stranglehold they had on me. Part three describes the practices that have kept me free and sane. I wish I could say I've never been haunted by issues of any kind once I dealt with them initially. But it's just not true.

My hope is that you find comfort in the fact that everyone who has a pulse has issues. And that in realizing you are not the only crazy person in the world, you will find not only comfort, but the courage to walk toward healing and freedom.

Part 2: The Process

Chapter 2
GI Joe

G.I. Joe is a smart man. When we were kids, my brother Jason and I had a daily ritual. After school each day we would grab a snack, grab a drink, migrate to the basement, and sit in front of the TV for a couple of blissful hours. We didn't simply watch mind-numbing cartoons. No, we sat at the feet of our animated guru, our illustrated wise one—G.I. Joe.

Most people wrongly assume that G.I. Joe was simply an action, army cartoon character. Little do they know that ol' Joe doled out profound wisdom. At the end of each half-hour episode, Joe offered a tidbit of advice to "Timmy" or "Mary" or whoever the kid of the day happened to be. One day, when Timmy was about to run into the street without having first looked both ways (what a moron, right?), G.I. Joe appeared out of nowhere just in time to grab Timmy's arm and save him from being flattened by a Mack truck. Then in a stern yet kind voice Joe said, "Timmy, you must always look both ways before crossing the street." Timmy replied, "Gee, thanks G.I. Joe. Now I know!" Joe would say, "Timmy," (and then his famous, always repeated line) "knowing is half the battle." Roll credits. End of show.

Who knew G.I. Joe was so wise? Knowing is half the battle.

My path to healing began with the work of discovering the source of my issues, in other words, with discovering my wounds. To be free I had to know. Because knowing is half the battle. You can't heal what you can't feel. Nice phrase. I didn't come up with it first, but it captures the first step toward healing a broken heart.

I remember when I was a sophomore in high school playing safety for the Gwinn Modeltowners. We were up against the Marquette Redmen. Early in the game they fumbled the ball. Reaching across my body, my left hand was the first hand to touch that football. Unfortunately a rather hefty fellow arrived soon after my hand did. He dove on the ball and thus my arm. Bam! Crack! Pop! My arm snapped in half like a twig.

I stood and saw the middle of my forearm bend into a 90 degree angle with my hand dangling. Had I been watching a YouTube video, it would have been awesome. Since it was my own arm, it was awful. I was rushed to the local hospital. The orthopedic surgeon had been called in while I was on the way. We met in the ER. What followed was without question the most grueling, intense pain I've ever felt. And much of the pain was caused by the doctor! That bonehead actually touched my broken arm. Can you believe it!

I about passed out when he touched it. After poking my arm he took me into the operating room, put me to sleep, cut me open, and screwed some plates in. Ouch. I awoke to absolute misery. I was livid with the doctor. Why did he have to touch the arm? Why did he have to cut me? It hurt like heck. His palpating, cutting, and screwing actually made it hurt worse. I cursed him for the knucklehead that he was and wished out loud that he had left me alone and never touched my broken arm.

What would have happened if that doctor had never touched my wound? What if he had listened to my cries and decided to not probe? I would have been crippled for the rest of my life. His probing, palpating, cutting, and screwing saved my arm. I can't imagine trying to type this story (let alone go through the rest of life) with one hand. At the time I thought he was a bonehead. In reality he was a miracle worker. A healer. You can't heal what you can't feel.

While at work a number of years ago, my friend Matt stepped on a nail. It went through his boot right into his foot. Matt panicked. He knew that as a diabetic he was prone to infection. He was scared to look. So instead of taking the time to look at the wound, touch it, probe it, clean it, he ignored the pain as best he could and acted as if it didn't happen, hoping it would go away. Six months later doctors removed the lower half of his leg.

It gets worse. A couple of years after having lost his right foot, Matt stepped on a staple in his living room with his left foot. Same thing. Same result. The doctors removed the lower half of that leg too. What's tragic is that both legs could have been saved had Matt taken time to touch the wound and deal with it. But he didn't. And he has no legs. You can't heal what you can't feel.

What's true for physical pain is true for emotional pain. If you can't feel it you can't heal it. Hearing that while in my therapist's office, I was dumbfounded. I had no idea where my issues came from. Steve (my counselor) told me that my first task was to discover the source of the pain. To do that, he recommended keeping a journal, writing down what was happening in my life. Finding the source of the junk was the beginning of feeling. Feeling leads to healing. In an effort to discover the root of my issues I began to carry around a journal.

Chapter 3
Present Passions

For two weeks I traveled everywhere with my trusty little journal in tow. I wrote about what was happening every time I got angry, sad, overly happy, or felt strongly in any way. I recorded my **present passions**.

One that I wrote about was actually a recurring passion. Every night when it was time to tuck my three little boys in bed, I had an irresistible urge to hug them, kiss them, tell them I loved them, and sing to them. I couldn't help myself. It had to be done. There was no way my boys were going to go to bed without a whole bunch of lovin' from me. Clearly this was a present passion, and I wrote about it in my trusty journal.

Another present passion that I recorded came on a Sunday morning. Kristy asked me to get the boys ready for church. Jake, Max, and Zeke wanted to wear flip flops to church that day. It was summer. It was warm. Why not, I thought. After all, didn't Jesus wear sandals? As Kristy came downstairs and saw the boys wearing flip flops, she asked, "Is it okay for them to wear flip flops to church?"

Instantly I hit the roof. To say I was livid would be an understatement. "What do you mean is it okay for them to wear flip flops! Of course it is! Church isn't about the outside, it is about the inside! How can you ask such a thing! Jesus wore sandals!"

I yelled and yelled. Passionately. Afterward I felt like an idiot. It wasn't as if she had asked to date other men. For crying out loud, she was just asking if flip flops were okay at our fairly conservative church. A gross overreaction on my part. Another present passion to jot down in that little journal.

I was on the path to healing, but noting my present passions would not be enough to get me there.

Chapter 4
Windows to Wounds

Having collected several moments of passion—some positive, like loving my kids, others negative, like yelling at Kristy—I was ready to take the next step toward freedom. My next assignment was to ask, What is behind those moments of passion? I learned that **present passions are windows to wounds.**

Most of my strong reactions were coming out of some painful event in my past. Asking what was behind a moment of passion was crucial to discovering the place of woundedness inside me. Examining a passionate moment is like having a doctor's hands-on exploration of an injury, probing for the problem.

It didn't take long to discover what was behind showing lots of love to my boys. The things I couldn't stop doing—hugging, kissing, affirming—were the very things I longed for from my own dad but didn't receive. He certainly wasn't mean. He wasn't at all abusive. He was emotionally absent.

He taught my brother Jason and me how to hit, throw, and shoot, but very rarely would he hug us, kiss us, or say "I love you." My little soul was like a dried-up sponge longing for Dad to throw some water my way. This present passion was a window into a very deep wound. At the time I realized the wound behind the passion I was in my early thirties, but I felt like a little boy dying for a touch or a loving word from Dad. My irresistible urge to be gushy with my boys came (and comes) right out of my longing for my dad to be gushy with me.

What about the flip flops? The wound behind that passion became readily apparent too. I had fallen in love with Jesus at a very early age (thanks, Mom!). For a time, the church was a wonderful place for me. But as I grew into my God-given personality and developed my own sense of style, it became clear that I didn't really "fit" in church. I liked my hair long. The church men liked theirs short. I hated suits (still do). Suits were a part of the uniform. I liked moving around—a lot. You had to sit still at church—very still. I just didn't seem to fit.

In college I worked at a Christian book store. One day I was listening to some heavier-than-usual Christian music. As I said, I liked my hair long. And I had an earring (just one back then). This woman walked into the store, heard the music, spotted me behind the counter, and with a look of utter contempt said, "I thought this was a Christian store!" She walked out, slamming the door behind her.

After graduating from seminary I was hired as an associate pastor at a large church in Kalamazoo, Michigan. An evaluation I received a couple years into my time there was pretty hurtful. Mind you, it wasn't just anyone who filled out the evaluation. It was the elders and other pastors—people commissioned to care for me and protect me. On the evaluation they noted that my pants were too baggy. My shirts were too bright (I do like orange). And my shirts were too drab (I do like brown). Hurtful and contradictory! I was told point-blank that I didn't look like a pastor.

Shortly after that I received a wonderful Matthew 18 letter: the if-you-have-a-problem-with-a-brother-go-to-him kind of letter. This woman modeled the Matthew 18 principle, asking to meet with me so the air would be clean between us. Very cool. The problem she had with me, however, was not cool. By this time my beloved long hair had fallen out on top so I was shaving my head, joining in with the work the Lord was already doing on the top of my dome. The woman's problem with me was that I looked like a drug dealer, and there was no way anyone over fifty would ever be able to respect me looking the way I did. Ouch. Wounds. No wonder I exploded when Kristy asked about the flip flops. She was unknowingly rubbing up against some painful places.

Now I knew my wounds. And knowing was half the battle.

Chapter 5
Lies Lie in Our Wounds

My grandpa used to tell lots of stories. He was an air force pilot and had a bunch of stories to tell. One story that I will never forget is of the time he was transporting wounded soldiers back to the States during the Korean War.

He told me how these soldiers with nasty, deep cuts would be carted onto the plane with their wounds filled with maggots. Yes, I said maggots. Maggots. In their wounds. Disgusting.

I remember sitting at his feet as a young boy, both sickened and intrigued. "Why maggots, Grandpa?" "Robbie," he would say, "I asked the same question. The medics told me that many a young man would lose a limb after having suffered a relatively minor wound. It wasn't the wound that got 'em. It was the infection. The maggots ate the infection right out of the wound. Cleaned those boys right up."

Hmmm…who knew? It wasn't the wound that got 'em. It was the infection.

Jesus calls Satan the father of lies. In other words, when Satan lies he's speaking his native language. Satan is a liar. A very good liar. His lies were deadly infections in the wounds of my heart. **Lies lie in our wounds**.

My dad, for a number of reasons, was not an affectionate guy. That was wounding. Yet it wasn't that wound that got me. As Grandpa said, it was the infection that got me. That infection was the lies Satan whispered into my heart over the years: "Your dad doesn't love you." "If you were worth anything your dad would hug you." "You are unlovable." "What a freak you are." "What is wrong with you? Your own dad won't even give you a kiss." "Reject." "Loser." "Shouldn't have been born." I listened to those lies. I believed them. And they were killing me.

Of course I was crazy about showing and speaking affection to my boys. I was driven by something very deep down. While the actions themselves were awesome, I was motivated out of my pain and out of my fear that my kids would grow up feeling unloved.

What about that evaluation I received at church? I looked like a drug dealer. Who cares? So what if my pants were too baggy? What's the big deal with being told you don't look like a pastor? In and of themselves, these words are mildly hurtful wounds. However with Satan's lies infecting those wounds, their pain was magnified a thousand-fold. "You have nothing to offer the church." "Who do you think you are, working in a church?" "You've wasted your life going to seminary." "What a useless waste of money you are." "You don't belong there at all." "You are stupid for thinking God would call you to be a pastor."

Kristy's innocent and valid question about the flip flops was like sticking a finger in a highly infected and painful wound. The lies were in deep.

By this time in my process, several months had passed, and I was exhausted. Uncovering the lies that I had bought into was crucial. But praise God, it wasn't the end. There was one more step I had to take to be free.

Chapter 6
Listening

At this point in my pursuit of freedom, some teaching I had received several years prior proved to be immeasurably valuable. So let me take a brief detour from the process to highlight something very helpful.

Someone once told me that if I trained the "ears" of my heart, I could hear the voice of the Lord. My heart having ears didn't line up with my high school biology, but this person was telling me that the Holy Spirit is God's voice in this world, and God wants to speak to me. This person also said that all those times in the Bible when God speaks to people are not exceptions, they are examples.

When Elijah was up on the mountain listening for the voice of God, he didn't hear God in the powerful wind that tore the mountain apart. God wasn't in the earthquake that shook the mountain or the fire that scorched it, either. Elijah heard God in a gentle whisper. God's voice. A still, small voice.

Jesus says that his sheep know his voice (John 10:27). He says the sheep listen for his voice and he calls them out by name. The sheep won't follow a stranger, because they don't know the stranger's voice, but they will follow the Good Shepherd because they know his voice.

His voice. He speaks. To us. His voice. The Spirit. Jesus said that the Father would send us the Counselor, the Holy Spirit, to teach us and remind us of all that Jesus said (John 14:26). His voice.

The apostle Paul teaches us to train ourselves in godliness (1 Timothy 4:7). So, to train myself in godliness and with the knowledge that God wanted to speak to me, I made my way to a nearby monastery to hear what God would say to me.

While hanging out in monksville, I set aside a half-hour to be still before the Lord. With journal on lap and pen in hand, I asked, What would you say to me, Lord? Instantly I wondered what was for dinner. Then I berated myself for not focusing, asked the question again, and focused. Another thought came: I wondered if the Pistons were going to play better next time. I berated myself for not focusing and asked the question again: What would you say to me, Lord? A thought flashed through my head: Does my belt match my shoes? Argh! I again berated myself for not focusing and asked the question again, and focused. This went on for twenty-nine and three-quarter minutes. When my time was almost up, something happened. I "heard" the words, "I love you, my boy."

When I say I heard them it wasn't as if I heard a voice speak out loud; it was like I was hearing a voice in my mind. And what I heard brought a rush of peace. Was that the voice of the Good Shepherd? I believe it was.

As the months and years went by and the work of training my "ears" continued, I got to the place where I could discern whether I was hearing my own voice, the voice of the father of lies, the voice of the world, or the still, small voice of the Holy Spirit. Four checks were helpful:

1. I had to check the words I had heard next to Scripture. They had to agree with what I read in the Bible.
2. I would often share the words with a godly brother or sister and ask for their feedback.
3. I had to pay attention to whether the words brought anxiety or anger or whether they brought peace and comfort.
4. Over time I could check whether the words had helped me heal.

By the time I started my journey to freedom, I was fairly familiar with the voice of the Lord. This was monumentally crucial in my healing. It was pivotal in the last step I had to take to be free.

In fact it was so foundational to my freedom, I recommend that you start training your heart's ears right now if they are not already trained to hear the still, small voice.

Your freedom just might depend on your ability to hear the wonderful, healing voice of the Counselor. More on this in a later chapter.

OK, back to the process.

Chapter 7
Truth Transforms

While Satan is the father of lies, Jesus says that he is the truth (John 14:6). He also says the truth will set us free (John 8:32). The truth will set us free. Freedom through truth. Sounds good, doesn't it?

Having unearthed the lies that were hidden deep in the wounds of my soul, I was ready to take that last step to freedom. Once again I picked up my trusty journal and made my way to the local monastery. I sat in my favorite place, wrote down each lie I had been believing, and asked God, "OK, what do you have to say about this one? Are these thoughts about my dad not loving me true or are they lies?" I heard a resounding, "Absolutely they are lies!"

God said, "They are lies from the pit of hell. I want you to know the truth, my boy. The truth is your dad loves you very much. In fact not only does he love you, he is proud of you. His lack of saying so is no reflection on you or his lack of love, rather it is a reflection of his own woundings from when he was a kid. Your dad didn't receive from his parents the stuff you want from him. He was doing the best he could with what he had. Remember he has a pulse too. He loves you a whole lot. And by the way, so do I."

Bam! I felt like Moses on the mountain. I felt like Elijah on the mountain. I was Rob on the mountain! God spoke to me and his truth set me free. His **truth transformed** my soul in a heartbeat. At that very moment, I was free. No longer was I haunted with old lies that were stuck in old wounds. I was free!

Highly encouraged and expectant, I then asked, "What about all that stuff I'd heard about my appearance and not belonging in the church? Truth or lies?" Again the answer was quick and resounding: "Lies. Lies from the pit of hell used to keep you down, for the kingdom of darkness knows you have a lot to offer. You are like Strider..." At this point the image of Strider from *The Lord of the Rings* came to my mind. He's scruffy looking. So much so that at first the hobbits were scared of him. Yet he was the one they needed to lead them to a place of safety so that they could continue on with the journey and complete the mission.

I heard the still, small voice say, "Without Strider the hobbits wouldn't have made it. I need you to lead the church. I need you to lead my people. You are my Strider." Amazing. I then heard the Spirit say, "I made you with your style and personality. That which has been a detriment (appearance) will become an asset. Be bold, Strider. Lead my people."

And that was it. I was free! Free as a bird. I heard the Spirit of the Lord speak his truth to me. Truth transforms. It takes one thing and changes it into something else. Literally. In a moment, God's truth transformed my wounds, my liabilities, into assets. God not only loves me as I am, God made me as I am to lead his people.

I packed up, drove home, and walked in the door. Kristy was in the kitchen making spaghetti. She took one look at me and asked, "What happen to you?" Then she laughed. She could tell just by looking at me that I was different. She could see I was free. The truth truly had set me free. The truth had transformed my wounded soul. I was healthy. I was free. I am healthy. I am free. Free is fun!

PP – WW – LL –TT
Present Passions are Windows to Wounds.
Lies Lie in our wounds. Truth Transforms.

Your assignment (it took me months; for you, it might take less time, it might take more time):

1. Record your "present passions."
2. Ask yourself, "What wounds are my present passions showing me?"
3. Sit with the Father and ask to see the lies that are lying in your wounds.
4. Ask the Spirit to speak his truth to you so that your wounds can be transformed.

Part 3: Free

Chapter 8
Junk Drawer

Everybody has one and nobody I know likes theirs. It's found in virtually every home, and in every home it evokes at least some level of stress. I'm talking about the family junk drawer.

Yours might be in a desk. It might be in a workroom. It could be in the cabinet in the sunroom. Our junk drawer is in the kitchen. And it's aptly named. Junk. In a drawer. Junk drawer. Kristy opens it and only shudders once. I open it and fall to the ground with convulsions. (My anal-retentive quotient is a bit higher than hers.) Neither of us likes it. Yet day after day, week after week, month after month, and year after year, we find ourselves the not-so-proud owners of a junk drawer.

It's not like we haven't cleaned it. In fact we've cleaned it numerous times. I can't tell you how many times we have pulled that sucker out, sorted, filed, thrown away, and restacked stuff, and reinserted that stupid drawer. There have been so many times I have lost count. Stupid drawer. It keeps on collecting junk.

As we've wrestled with the junk drawer, we've realized that cleaning it is only half the work. And work it is. It isn't easy sorting, cleaning, etc. It takes time, effort, and energy. Yet cleaning up in and of itself will not keep our junk drawer free. No, it takes more. More effort. More energy. More time. More, more, more. *Ipso facto*. After the fact. After the drawer has been tidied it must been tended to regularly if that tidiness is to be kept. The cleaning event isn't enough. It must be coupled with some long-term drawer care.

Life is like a junk drawer.

It would be awesome if, after having walked through a process to freedom, I never again was confronted with deep wounds and pains. It would be wonderful if I could say the lies of the enemy never again affected me.

It would be great, but it is just not reality. In this life you will have troubles. If you have a pulse, you have issues. The following chapters are filled with tools or disciplines I have used in order to "keep the junk drawer clean." They are only tools. Means to an end. Not the end in themselves. Just tools. Maybe you'll find some of them helpful.

Chapter 9
Voodoo

I Googled "voodoo." Here's what I found:

> This is what our clients are saying at CaliforniaAstrology.com. Every single one of these testimonials is absolutely real.

They must be, 'cause I'm reading it online, right?

> These testimonials are sent to us by clients all over the world.

Are you ready to hear testimonials from voodoo clients from California Astrology? Check this out. This from Kathy in California:

> Dear CAA, In February of 2002, I ordered two spells, one from Andrakka and one from Burton. I also ordered two Wanga Dolls [close relatives of voodoo dolls], one for money and one for luck. Two months later in May, I was on the brink of suicide and had just about given up on life when I received $15,000 from an unlikely source to help me turn my life around. I know in my heart that all of what I ordered from CAA greatly contributed to my still being alive. I received it because I did the spell.

Did you get that? This woman had junk in her life. She has a pulse, therefore she must have issues. So she ordered this spell where all she had to do was steps a, b, c, and d, with no real thought of her own, no real investment of her own; she just had to pay the money, do a, b, c, and d, and life was great.

What about this testimonial from Becky?

You guys cast a retrieval lovers' spell for me back in February and I'd like to thank you for it. My ex and I have been back together for a month now.

Amazing! Voodoo. Do you get this voodoo? This is pretty sweet! All you got to do is order the spell that you need and with no real effort—you just go through steps a, b, c, d, and maybe e—and voila! Things are perfect. Or if you don't even want to put that amount of work into it, just pay the professional to do it for you. Just pay them; they'll do it for you, and your life will be great.

Enough of this voodoo stuff for a minute. Let me ask you this: Do you have a pulse? Then you must have issues. Hopefully, we have established that by now. We've all got issues. How many of you would like greater peace and joy in the midst of life? Well, if you want peace and joy in the midst of life all you got to do is come to church on Sunday morning. You also must come to mid-week fellowship. You must serve in the nursery at least once a month. And of course, you must tithe. If you do these four things, steps a, b, c, and d, voila! Life will be good!

How many husbands would like to be a better husband? Or how many wives would love to be just a wonderful wife who blesses her spouse? All they have to do is steps a through d as outlined above. Their marriages will be sweet. I guarantee it.

Maybe someone would like to see the Lord work in the lives of her children? She doesn't have to do anything except pay me as the professional; I'll do the praying on her behalf, and her kids will be fine, right?

Here's the thing. We've taken this thing called Christianity and unknowingly, and probably without even wanting to, boiled it down and pared it down until we've made it nothing more than Christian voodoo. And we interact with it, with Jesus, just like those people ordering wanga dolls. If we just show up and do a, b, c, and d, then everything will be fine. If we just invest here, here, and here, then things will be great. Stand up, sit down, kneel, raise your hands, come to study group, tithe. If you do this and this and this, everything is going to be fine.

It's Christian voodoo, and we see it all over. Sometimes I see it in the mirror. It's so easy to go through the motions. What do you do on

Sundays? I go to church.

So, in the rest of this book we are going to make sure that we have nothing to do with Christian voodoo. We're going to go back to the basics of what Christianity is about. What its exact point is.

Raise your right hand, wiggle your fingers, and say, "Hi, this is me." Then raise your left hand and say, "This is the Lord." Then clasp your two hands together and say, "This is the point of Christianity."

This is what it's about. The point of it all is for us to be close, intimate, tight with the Father through the work of the Son because of the Holy Spirit. This is the point of Christianity. The King of kings, the Lord of lords, the creator of the universe, took the nails and came out of the tomb, made it an empty tomb. Why? So that we could go through the motions of religious practice? No! So that we could be joined with him!

If you don't believe me, maybe you'll believe the Word of God. Throughout the Scriptures, if you just canvass the Scriptures, you'll see that God's purpose is for humans to be with him. Not to do a, b, c, and d so you'll get your prayers answered, but to walk hand in hand with him! Even in the Garden of Eden, when Adam and Eve had already sinned and walked away from God in disobedience, we see evidence of God's desire to be with us. The Lord came down to walk with Adam and Eve. Do you remember what time of day it was? The cool of the day. The Lord came down and walked through the garden with them in the cool of the day for one reason only, for fellowship. The cool of the day is when it's relaxed, the time of day you kick back, hang out on the porch, and watch the world go by together. You just sit down under a tree and chat in the cool of the day.

At the very beginning, God's plan was to be close to us, but of course Adam and Eve bit into that apple and walked away from God. Humans walked away from God, but God says, "No, I want to be close to you."

We see this when Jesus was speaking to his disciples in John 15:15, one of the most profound passages in the Bible. God, the one who created it all, the one who sustains the world with his breath, says, "I no longer call you servants...I have called you friends." God wants to be our friend. Unbelievable!

And this is important: God does not want us to go through any certain steps to get things from him. God simply wants us to be in tight connection with him.

Here's the key: say no to Christian voodoo and yes to walking closely with Jesus. It sounds simple and obvious, but sometimes the simple and obvious things are easily overlooked. This truth completely changed my walk with the Lord: God will speak to you if you listen.

God will speak to you if you listen. Certainly he'll speak to you through the Word, and through teaching, and through good songs; but I'm saying that he'll talk to you just like he talked to Adam and Eve. Boom! Just you and the Lord, through the Holy Spirit. You will hear from God if you listen.

And it wasn't just Adam and Eve. It was Abram. God said to Abram, "Get up and go," so he got up and went. Why? Because he had heard from God. Remember Noah? God said, "Build a boat." He said, "Okay." Why did he build a boat? Because God told him to. David. Paul. Timothy. All through the Scriptures, God's people heard the voice of the Lord through the Holy Spirit. Now, that's either a very cool bunch of exceptions, times of hearing God speak that were meant only for those people, or it's a very cool reality that you and I can walk in: God will speak to us.

Here's the point: God wants to speak to you through the Holy Spirit, and you need to train your inner ear to hear him. Sounds easy! Does the thought of God talking to you sound cool? God literally, through his Spirit, wants to speak specific things to you. Something just to you.

The bad news is that it's not as easy as it sounds. Darn! The Bible, in Psalm 46:10, says, "Be still, and know that I am God." If there was ever a verse that slams up against American culture, this is it. Be still, are you kidding me? Be still? Of course I want to hear the voice of the Lord. But *be still*?

The Bible, in 1 Kings, chapter 19, tells us that the prophet Elijah went up on Mount Horeb to meet with the Lord, and the lightning came, BOOM! But the Lord's voice was not there. Flames came, but the voice of God wasn't in the roaring flames. The earth shook, but the voice of the Lord was not in the earthquake. Instead, the voice of the Lord came in a whisper. Here's what I want for you. I want you to train your ears to hear the whisper of the Lord.

I've told how in the past I had an addiction to pornography and I wrestled with depression. I was a disciplined man, and I walked in discipline; but self discipline was not the way to freedom. Restoration was the way to freedom.

I got free from depression and addiction to pornography when I began to walk hand in hand with God.

Prayer

Lord, your Word tells us that we did not choose you but you chose us and appointed us to bear fruit, fruit that lasts. We declare by faith that you chose us and destined us to be your adopted children, according to your good pleasure. We declare that we are sons and daughters of the King. Therefore, we have an inheritance in your kingdom and we declare, Lord, that we want that kingdom to come and your will to be done here on earth as it is in heaven. Amen.

Go Deeper

→ What are your thoughts on this notion of "Christian voodoo"?

→ Where have you seen it in your life?

→ What would it look like for you to walk hand in hand with God?

→ Take time each day this week to train your inner ears to hear.

Chapter 10
Father

When Jesus' disciples asked him to teach them how to pray, he began, "Our Father..." At the moment he could reveal anything about the nature of God—when he could have said "Our Creator" or "Our Provider" or "Our Sustainer"—what Jesus chose to reveal about God is this thing called fatherhood. God is Abba. Our Father.

What does it mean for God to be revealed to us as Father?

The word "father" has been messed up over the years. How many of you have encountered deep pain and wounds from a father? There are wonderful places we can point to for good examples of fatherhood, but in our world, unfortunately, there are a million examples of what a father should not be.

For whatever reason, in our culture men are taught to be firm and strong, with a stiff upper lip. Never to show emotion. That might be okay at some points, but when you're a little kid and you long to see emotion and affection from Dad, the absence of it is deadly.

Men in our culture are under all kinds of pressure, and sometimes that pressure is relieved by having an affair with hobbies. So, many kids grow up with a father who is absent—out doing his own thing to recharge his own batteries. It's as if their kids are a secondhand thought. We come from fathers who have issues of their own. So while our fathers are sometimes doing the best that they can, the best that they can do is not close to what we need.

So when Jesus teaches his followers to pray beginning "Our Father," it can leave us scratching our heads and asking, *What in the world does it mean for God to be father?* Does it mean that he is absent and distant? That he's engaged elsewhere but not with me? That I'm a secondhand thought to Abba?

Unintentionally, maybe even unknowingly, many of us treat God the Father like the fathers we've seen on earth. How many of us when we are sick, not feeling well, have prayed: "Father, if it's your will, bring healing"? Have you ever said that? "If it's your will." If you've been jobless, have you approached prayer this way? Or in your gut thought, If it's your will, give me a job. How many of us, in a lonely time when we just long for someone to call "friend," have prayed, "If it's your will, bring me somebody"?

Jesus taught his disciples to pray "Father...your will be done."

Well, how do we know the will of the Father? And how do we know the heart of the Father? What Jesus taught his followers is very helpful in answering these questions. The will of the Father and the heart of the Father are revealed in Jesus. The apostle John has recorded Jesus speaking in John chapter 14, verse 6. Jesus says, "I am the way, and the truth, and the life. No one comes to the Father except through me." Jesus also says, "If you really know me, you will know my Father as well." If you really know me, Jesus says, you know my father as well. And he adds, "From now on you do know him and have seen him."

Then Philip, one of the disciples, says, "Lord, show us the Father and that will be enough for us." Jesus answers, "Don't you know me, Philip, even after I have been among you such a long time? Anyone who has seen me has seen the Father. How can you say, 'Show us the Father'?"

"Anyone who has seen me has seen the Father." How do we know the very will and the very heart of the Father? By looking at Jesus. If we want a clear picture of what it means for God to be Abba, if we want to know the heart of Abba, all we need to do is look at Jesus.

In Luke, chapter 18, we get another glimpse of the Father's heart. The disciples are walking along and a group of kids cries out to Jesus: "Jesus, Jesus!" The disciples rebuke them: Get the children away; he's a busy man. So we've got these underdogs, these underprivileged beings known as children, screaming out to the one who represents God the Father.

Now imagine Jesus saying, "Shut those kids up, please. I'm busy. I have things to do. Don't bother me with these little children with their snotty noses."

What does it feel like in your gut when you read that? It's not right. When these powerless, culturally voiceless children cried out to Jesus, as busy as he was, on a mission from God, he took a time-out. Because they *were* his mission. They *were* his business. He says, "Let the children come to me." Jesus has a soft spot in his heart for kids.

So, according to John 14 we can assume that the Father does as well.

In Ephesians 1:5 (NRSV), the apostle Paul says: "[God] destined us for adoption as his children through Jesus Christ, according to the good pleasure of his will." John writes in 1 John 3:1 (NRSV): "See what love the Father has given us, that we should be called children of God." The heart of Jesus was for children and therefore the heart of the Father is for children. I don't care how old you are, you're a kid in the eyes of the Lord. And I don't care how arthritic and crippled you are or how much your back hurts, the Lord says, "Come and sit in my lap, for you are mine."

Zacchaeus. He was a wee little man, a wee little man was he. Do you know the story? It's in Luke, chapter 19. Zacchaeus was a knucklehead sinner; he had issues. He had a pulse, so he had issues. He was a Jewish man employed by the government in Rome to steal from and cheat his own people. He was excited to see Jesus, so he climbed up a sycamore tree because he was a short man. Obviously he had no friends, right? Because a friend would have said, "Come on over here so you can see, little guy."

Now imagine Jesus walking up to Zacchaeus, sticking his finger in his face, and saying: "I don't like your behavior, Zacchaeus. You need to get down on your knees and say the Lord's Prayer ten times, give to the temple, and get your act together before I'll have anything to do with you."

No, that's not right at all. To Zacchaeus, to this man stuck in his sin, stuck in indulgent, self-centered living, Jesus says, "Come on down, homie, I'm going to kick it at your house today! Even before you do anything to make your life right, I love you. And I'm going to show you that I love you by hanging out with you. Now, let's go eat some food."

Maybe you don't have issues like Zacchaeus. You don't cheat, steal, plunder, or live selfishly. But supposing we have other kinds of sin issues. (We really don't have to suppose, do we?) Aren't Jesus' words really good news? Because when we see Jesus treat a sinful man with love and open arms, we see the reality of Abba. The Father loves us in spite of our stupidity and sinfulness.

John, chapter 8, tells about a woman caught in adultery. Jewish religious leaders dragged her in front of Jesus to shame her and to see what he would do. According to the ancient text, the Old Testament, a man or a woman caught in adultery was worthy of death by stoning. But in John, chapter 8, Jesus says to the woman, "Hey, I don't condemn you." He stands between her and the religious shame that was coming her way and he deflects the shame the others were throwing on her. Then he says, "Okay, now get up and dust yourself off. I don't condemn you. Go and sin no more." Because we see the way Jesus treated a shame-filled woman, we know the Father's heart toward the shame-filled is peace and grace. Amen!

John, chapter 4, tells about a woman who had had five husbands. Politically and socially, she was a complete outcast. Jesus sat down next to her at a well at high noon. She was there in the hottest part of the day because no other woman wanted to be near her. Jesus asked her for a drink of water, and in presenting his need to her, he touched her need for community and for grace and forgiveness. So seeing how Jesus reached out to the outcast, to the loner, to the one who is filled with remorse and shame, we see the heart of the Father. Friends, if that is your story, know that there is a Father who loves you.

In Luke, chapter 4, Jesus addresses brokenhearted people. Does he say, "I've come to teach you a lesson: you're brokenhearted because of your own poor choices?" No. He says, "I've come to heal the brokenhearted." That's what it says in Luke 4. It does not say, "I've come to heal the brokenhearted once they get their act together and say that they're sorry for all that they've done." Jesus' heart for the brokenhearted is for healing. John 14 tells us that when we see Jesus, we see the Father. The Father is for the brokenhearted.

What about Matthew, chapter 5, where it says that those who mourn, those who hunger and thirst for righteousness, those who are poor in spirit will be blessed? Jesus is for the underdog. He's not necessarily tooting the horn for those with power and prestige. Although he loves them too, he really has a heart for the underdog. Do you ever feel like you're an outsider, like you have no power, no voice, life always stinks, you're always down, and things are never going right for you? Then you are in just the right place to receive the love of Jesus, and therefore the love of Abba, because the Father is for you and loves you.

Let's look at what Jesus did on behalf of exploited poor people. Many of us when we were growing up saw pictures of Jesus with a sheep around his shoulders or with kids all around him—gentle Jesus. But have you ever seen the picture of Jesus throwing the tables over in the temple and snapping a whip—angry Jesus? Have you seen that picture on a church wall? Because this angry Jesus is an accurate picture of the reaction of Jesus and the Father when God's children are exploited.

You see, in John, chapter 2, when Jesus cleared out of the temple the people who were selling animals for sacrifice and the moneylenders, it was because he was angry that these people were picking on his kids. The people coming to the temple to worship were poor and had little means, yet they were being exploited by people who were selling, at ridiculously high prices, the things these poor people needed to be able to worship. Jesus said, "Not in my house!"

So if you've ever felt exploited, used, abused, know that it stirs up anger, a righteous anger, that burns in the heart of the Father, because we see that in the heart of his son, Jesus.

What about sick people? What did Jesus do with sick people throughout the Scriptures? Did he say, "Oh, you're sick? Hang on, let me pray for a minute and discern the Father's will on how I should pray for you. Lord, is it your will to heal Judy? Okay. Sorry, Judy. Not today. Lord, is it your will to heal Dale? Okay, yes, we'll heal Dale. But not Judy. I'm sorry, John. Drew, no. Not the Father's will for you. Stacy! It's your lucky day. Yes, you win the lottery today. The Lord is going to bring you healing. Chandler, you're hosed. Sorry, nothing. It's not the Father's will today." Is this what Jesus did when he encountered sick people?

How many sick people that Jesus encountered did he not heal? Zero. He healed every person who came to him and asked for healing. He did not need to take a time-out and seek the Father's will, because Jesus knew the will of the Father, and that was to bring his kingdom. Wherever the kingdom of God was, there was no sickness—there is no sickness.

So, it is good and it is right for us to say to God, "Happy Father's Day." Because he's good and his heart and his will are for us. God is for you. We wrestle with it: Is it God's will for me to be well? Is it God's will for me to have this job? Is it God's will for me to have a fulfilling life? Somewhere along the line we've come to believe that God wants us to live as paupers, just getting by. He said, "I have come that they may have life... to the full" (John 10:10).

By the time I was thirty-two years old, I had torn my ACL three times, had four reconstructive knee surgeries, and broken my ankles several times. A well respected orthopedic surgeon told me, "Hey, you better take up shuffleboard." I was thirty-two! Well, I began believing this teaching that God wants us to be healed, so we had people pray, right? What happened the first time we prayed? Nothing. The second time? Nothing. But the third time that we prayed for the kingdom to come, the pain in my knees and ankles was gone. Totally gone.

I used to be an insomniac. You know, tired all day, go to bed wide awake. Ambien was my friend. Man, some funky things happened to me on Ambien. I went to the gym one morning, came to work later, and was like, did I go to the gym this morning? I had no recollection of having gone to the gym. So I went out to the car; sure enough my gym clothes were wet and sweaty.

That was scary. So I said, "Lord, I want your healing." Now I sleep like a baby—I scream and wet the bed. Just kidding. I sleep like a rock. All through the night.

Zoloft also was my friend for depression for a long time. But after good therapy, good processes from the Lord, and a healing prayer, I am depression free.

The will of the Father is for you.

Prayer

Father, we are broken and wounded people. We feel the brokenness of life. Lord, you reveal yourself through your son and through the Holy Spirit as Abba, Father, Dad. Lord, we ask that you would give us a fresh and right understanding of what that means.

Kind, strong, compassionate, affectionate, loving, sacrificing Lord, I pray for a touch from Abba. From Dad. Lord, you say to each of us, "You are my son, you are my daughter, and I love you. You are very precious and dear to me. I think a lot of you. I have a lot for you."

"You're my boy, you're my girl," says the Lord. Come, Holy Spirit. You know exactly what each of us needs, and for that we say thank you. Amen.

Go Deeper

→ What images come to your mind when you hear the word "father"?

→ How might the realization of God as "Father" be an instrument in your freedom?

Chapter 11
Pulse

Let's revisit a statement you've come across a few times by now.

If you have a pulse, you have issues.

That's reality because we live in a broken world where broken people do stupid things that hurt others. This is a biblical truth. We see Joseph in the Old Testament; he's the dude who had a coat of many colors. Check out the story if you've never read it. It starts in Genesis, chapter 37. Joseph's brothers were jealous of him, and in their sinfulness and brokenness they sold him into slavery. The man had issues; he was brokenhearted because his brothers had deeply wounded him.

What about King David? The man had issues, right? He was the king of all kings on the earth, could have anything he wanted—except another man's wife. But because of his own stupid choices and his own sinfulness, he did some things that were really bad: slept with another man's wife, killed him, and covered it up. The man had issues.

Job was afflicted by Satan. If you don't know the story, he's got his own book in the Bible called Job. You don't have to read far into the book to see the work the enemy did in his life; the man had issues.

See, we're no different from these people we learn about in the Bible. They had issues; we have issues—either because of wounds inflicted by others, wounds inflicted by ourselves, or wounds inflicted by the kingdom of darkness. And I have doubts that we're deeply in tune with our own woundedness. Lots of people are out of touch with the reality that they have issues. That's a problem, because if we don't know about our wounds, we won't experience the depth of healing that we could from the One who wants to heal us.

And the reality is that our wounds lead us to do some dumb things, right? Because we're wounded, we sometimes shut down, we can even go dead inside. Our hearts can become cold and hard, like stone. In the book *The Wizard of Oz*, the Tin Man says, "The greatest loss I ever experienced was the loss of my heart." He says that no man or woman can love who doesn't have a heart.

You have a pulse, therefore you have issues. And one of the results of our issues, deep wounds, can lead us to live like the Tin Man, heartless. God created us with a heart, and we want to live as God intended. But when we're wounded and dead inside, we don't know how to live. We chase after things that can, for a while, seem to give us life, but in reality it's a hollow echo of the life the Lord has for us. We run after drugs, alcohol, pornography, careers, trying to awaken our dead, stone hearts. Or we find ways to isolate ourselves; we don't want to be around people.

Maybe we hide behind anger; we explode for no reason, and we say things that we know we don't mean, but we can't seem to help it because we're dead inside. We have anger issues because of our woundedness. The list is long. Do you know the symptoms of your issues? Because in order to ask God to heal your wounds, you have to admit that they're there.

Have you ever heard someone say that life stinks and then you die? Well, in a way, they're right. It's a good description of a life lived apart from God. Life stinks. Maybe you experience a little joy once in a while, and then you die.

But God's Word has something to say to us about our deadness and our stone-heartedness. In the book of Ezekiel, chapter 11, verse 19, it says, "I will give [the people of Israel] an undivided heart and put a new spirit in them; I will remove from them their heart of stone and give them a heart of flesh."

God is speaking to the Israelites, God's chosen people. Who are God's chosen people today? Israel was then, but it's expanded a little. Who are God's chosen people today? We are! We are Christ's chosen people. John, chapter 15, verse 16, in the New Testament, tells us that Jesus says, "You did not choose me but I chose you. And I appointed you to go and bear fruit, fruit that will last" (NRSV). Jesus chose us to be his kids. And so when we read in the Old Testament about God's chosen people, by extension, through the Holy Spirit, we can say, "You know what? There are some things in there for me because I'm one of God's chosen people."

God's chosen people in this story in the book of Ezekiel are oppressed and enslaved. The nation of Babylon, led by King Nebuchadnezzar, strong and powerful, mighty as could be, swept in and took all of Israel's young, handsome people to Babylon, where they lived in exile and served as slaves. The Babylonians left all the Israelites who were poor behind. All of Israel's wealth went to Babylon.

You could say that the Israelites had a pulse, therefore they had issues. So the word of the Lord comes to the people through the prophet Ezekiel, to a bunch of people who have issues. The Lord says, "I will give them an undivided heart," in other words, a heart that's not broken. If it's divided, it's broken, right? The Lord says, "I will give them an undivided heart and put a new spirit in them; I will remove from them their heart of stone and give them a heart of flesh." Huh! Remove from them a heart of stone and give them a heart of flesh.

What the Lord is saying is that the Lord is going to bring healing and restoration and hope. The Lord says to a people ridden with issues, "I will bring restoration, healing, and hope." The Lord says, "I know you have issues. Others are oppressing you. Your own poor choices and the kingdom of darkness are leading to your wounds and your issues, but I will come down and heal that broken heart. I'll give you an undivided heart. You won't chase things anymore that don't mean anything, and I will bring restoration. I'll give you a heart that is flesh and not stone."

The dead-of-heart will be alive-of-heart. They will have hearts that can feel again. "I will give them an undivided heart…I will remove from them their heart of stone and give them a heart of flesh." To anyone who understands that they have issues, this is good news!

When I think about this, I get emotional. I battled pornography for over fifteen years. Freedom is good! I was on Zoloft and wrestled with depression for the longest time, and freedom is good! When I was depressed and living a life of ups and downs, I had no idea I was depressed. I thought everything was great until someone told me, "Stop it! Look at yourself; you're miserable." Someone basically told me to look in the mirror and say, "You're pathetic." But he also said that Jesus came to set the pathetic free.

Pay attention because this is something that you just cannot miss. The Lord says, "I will give you a new heart. I'm going to take the dead one and remove it, and I'm going to give you a live heart that beats and brings the abundance of Jesus."

Do you want this new heart? Here's what I tell people at The River to do. You need to bring the worship pastor a diet Dr. Pepper and a sweatband every Sunday. You need to bring the executive pastor an ice cold Mountain Dew every Sunday, and of course, you need to bring me a Mountain Dew every Sunday, too. This is only the beginning of what you need to do to earn this freedom that the Lord has for you. You also better tithe at least fifteen percent of your income to the joy boxes. You better volunteer to work in the children's ministry; otherwise, kids will go to hell, and you might, too. You absolutely better shampoo the church carpets at least once a year. You have to attend the 9:30 or 11:00 worship service and serve on the hospitality team at one of the others. And you must come to the midweek service, too. Do all this, and you'll earn this new heart that the Lord has for you.

Wrong! In reality this beautiful thing, this newness of heart, this removing of the dead heart, it's nothing we can earn! The Lord says, "I will give them an undivided heart…I will remove their stone heart… and give them a heart of flesh." It's a gift from the Lord for us, so don't you even think about earning it! Think about receiving it!

God is in the business of healing broken hearts. Jesus quotes a prophecy in Isaiah 61 that says, "I've come to heal the brokenhearted." John 8 tells us that when everybody wanted to condemn the woman caught in adultery and shame her, Jesus said, "Hey, I don't condemn you. No! Go and sin no more." That's what Jesus did with Zacchaeus, right? The world would say, "You're an idiot, Zacchaeus. You've got issues. You stay in that tree." Jesus said, "Come on down." Put his arm around Zacchaeus and said, "We're going to go hang out." And in the hanging out, the man was set free.

Jesus is in the business of restoring people who need restoration and who can't restore themselves. Now if you've tried to restore yourself, you'll understand what good news this is. Because our own efforts don't work. We try harder. We might tithe more. We might shampoo the church carpets. We might try to do something in a Christian cosmic karma kind of way to earn stuff; it just doesn't work. We've tried self-help. We've tried more discipline. But none of that stuff works.

We don't need more discipline; we simply need more freedom, so stop working at it! Just crawl up in the lap of Abba. Jesus says in Matthew 11, "Come to me, all who are weary and burdened." I'll put that in my language. Jesus says, "Come to me if you got issues and are wounded, and I will give you"—what?—"rest. I'll give you rest." Rest. All you got to do, the Scriptures say, is go to him and sit with him, and he will give you rest. It's what Jesus is about throughout the Scriptures, old and new. In Galatians, chapter 5, the apostle Paul writes, "It is for freedom that Christ has set us free."

Without the healing work of Jesus we're pathetic. But because we can go to the one who says, "I will give you a heart of flesh and an undivided heart," because we can go to the one who gives us a new heart, who says, "Come to me and rest," we are not pathetic. We can be free.

We just need to respond to this good news that the Lord will give us new hearts; the Lord will meet us in our issues and bring us freedom. By "we" I mean those of us who have a pulse. Or if that's not clear enough, those of us with an ear on each side of our head and a nose in the middle of our face. I mean parents who get frustrated and confused about what to do with their kids. People who get uncontrollably enraged when they're driving down the highway and someone cuts them off.

People who can't kick an addiction to alcohol, drugs, or pornography. People who bury themselves in work all the time because they don't want to deal with something in their lives. I mean people whose marriages stink, who have kids who have gone away from the Lord, or who themselves are currently away from the Lord. People who only go to church because somebody drags them there or they drag themselves there.

The Lord will remove your heart of stone and give you a new heart of flesh.

Prayer

Lord, you are Lord of lords. You are King of kings, creator of heaven and earth, sustainer of all life, the giver of all good things, Abba, Father. You love us like a father, like a mother loves her child. You are our God and we declare, Lord, that we need you and that we don't even know we need you. Lord, when we say we need you, we acknowledge that we don't even know how much we need you. Lord, we need you. We are yours. We belong to you. We declare this by faith. We are yours. Amen.

Go Deeper

→ What would the three people who are closest to you say your issues are?

→ Go ask them.

Chapert 12
Listen

Have you heard the story of Nadia Bloom? Eleven-year-old Nadia Bloom disappeared in Seminole County, Florida, in April 2010. The people searching for her were close to throwing in the towel. For four days they'd looked throughout the dense, swampy terrain near Nadia's home, and they could not find her.

Then, a dude from her church, James King, was praying in the evening, as he always did, and he heard the voice of the Lord. As he was in his prayer time, God spoke to him: "We're going to find her." He'd trained his inner ear to hear God's voice, so he asked, "So, God, what are we going to do?" The Lord told him, "She's going to have a lot of bug bites. She's going to need water. Pack up your backpack, walk out your door tomorrow morning, and I will lead you to Nadia."

So the next morning James stepped out the door with his backpack and walked until he came to a stream. On CNN's website* he tells how he got to a stream and the Lord said, "Cross the stream." So he walked across it. He heard the voice of the Lord say, "Go east; follow the sun." So he followed the sun. The Lord directed his way, and in two hours he did what people had not been able to do in four days. He walked straight to young Nadia Bloom, and saved her life.

Unbelievable! When we hear the voice of the Lord, lost people who are headed toward death will be found and find life. Will you put in the time to train your inner ear? People right in our own churches who are lost will find life if we listen for God's direction and do what God asks us to do.

One week Kathryn played the piano for worship at our church, and we sang "This Little Light of Mine." Afterward, Kathryn came up to me and said, "This week I was praying and the Lord told me it was time to move to South Bend and reopen my catering business."

She went about her day and was at a women's gathering later that afternoon and shared how she had heard the voice of the Lord. She did

---

*www.cnn.com/video/?/video/us/2010/04/14/am.intv.swamp.rescuer.cnn

this with a little trepidation, because whenever you say you've heard the voice of the Lord, people can be skeptical. She said, "I think I heard the Lord tell me I'm supposed to move to South Bend and reopen my catering business. But I don't have anywhere to live in South Bend or any money to do this."

A woman across from her said, "Oh, I'm from South Bend, and I have a basement that has an apartment. You can come and live with me for free. You want to do that?"

And then the woman went on to say, "I've got a full-size, industrial kitchen in the basement. It's yours to use for your business."

When we hear from the Lord, amazing things happen! Do you want to hear the Lord? If you do, you gotta work at it. I've been married more than fifteen years. It's a great marriage, but we've had to work at our marriage. My friends often tell me that they're jealous of my marriage, and I tell them that they should be, because I've got a great wife and a great marriage. Well, we've worked at it. We've invested in each other. We've gotten away to spend time together. We've had some tough discussions. It's work! But it's worth it.

One of the most important things we've learned to do is listen—to the Lord and to each other. It's probably been a bigger adjustment for me than for my wife, because like a lot of guys, I've spent the years doing a lot more talking than listening. It's because—just in case you didn't realize it—men are different from women.

I was in Colorado a while back, up in the mountains at 13,000 feet. It's pretty up there. It was thirty-nine degrees and snowy. Just perfect. I was speaking to a large group of men at a men's conference. They had me come out there to speak, and I think they liked me. I think they were impressed with the profound, cutting-edge insight that I brought to the table. I told them that men are different than women. You too are astounded by that insight, right?

While there, I shared some research about a group of second-graders who were recorded for two weeks. For two weeks these kids' conversations were recorded all day at school, and then researchers evaluated what they had said. One hundred percent of what came from little girls' mouths was relational, in sentences like, "Oh, I like your hair today," or "Boy, that dress looks great," or "How are you today?" The researchers found that little girls, one hundred percent of the time, when they speak it's relational.

And then they analyzed what happened with little boys. Only sixty percent of what came out the boys' mouths could be called words. Forty percent of the time it was sounds like Whoosh! Whoosh! Boom! Bang! Pow! Of the sixty percent of boys' sounds that were actually words, the thoughts they expressed were more factual or competitive than relational. Things like, "I'm bigger than you" and "What have you got in your lunch?" The researchers were impressed with these differences between boys and girls. Men are different from women.

Anyway, back to my point.

Kristy and I have something new in our marriage. After fifteen and a half years of marriage we've decided that we are no longer going to listen to one another. So when she talks, all I hear is blah, blah, blah. And when I talk, you know what she hears? Blah, blah, blah. It's just amazing for us how it's changed the dynamic of our relationship. We no longer listen to one another. Oh, we still speak at one another, but we're done listening; we are not going to listen any more. And it's done such remarkable things for my marriage that I've taken it to my closest friendships. We've decided that we're done listening. It's over. Listening is overrated! We're just going to talk at one another, and if it looks like the other person's not listening we're just going to talk louder; but we're done listening. Listening—blegh!

You get the point, right? What would my marriage be like if that was true? Awful! I wouldn't have one. What would my friendships be like if we never listened to each other? It would be pathetic. They wouldn't be friendships. And maybe you know such people; maybe you're one of them, huh? Some people just talk, talk, talk, and they never listen. How much do you want to be in their company?

The Lord wants to speak to you. And it begins with training yourself to listen to hear the voice of the Lord. Years ago, when I learned that God would speak to me if I could be still and listen, I said to myself, I'd kind of like to hear from God. That'd be kind of cool, so I'm going to work at being still. I see that there are so many distractions in my world, so I'm going to work at being still. As the apostle Paul says it in 1 Timothy, chapter 4, "Train yourself to be godly."

So I decided to go down to Three Rivers once a month, to visit the monastery down there. I talked about this experience earlier, in Chapter 7. Seven monks live in a place called St. Gregory's Abbey. Man, they're a kickin' group of dudes. Crazy dudes, but I love them because they gave me a place to be silent.

So I went down there and spent some of the day reading. Then I said, "Okay, Lord." I had a journal and a pen; you might want to do the same if you want to train to hear. And I said, "Lord, what do you want to say to me today? I want to hear."

That's a good thought. I could hear a clock ticking. What did I start thinking about? *What's for dinner? What's for dinner?*

Focus! *Man, I'm still hungry.* Focus. Be still and know. This should be easy. *Man, the Pistons were awful last night.*

Oh, it's hard to be still and find quiet places. I was even thinking, *Does my belt match my shoes?* You see, the Lord will speak to us; but we've been so trained to have our minds always moving. It's almost impossible to sit and be still, to hear the voice of the Lord.

And yet, in the midst of that half-hour, with all my jumbled, goofy old thoughts, I heard, *I love you.* I love you? That wasn't me. I don't tell myself I love me. Was that God? And so, month after month, I would go back and sit for a half-hour down at St. Gregory's Abbey in Three Rivers, Michigan, and say, "Lord, I want to hear from you because I'm tired of my prayer life and my faith life being undisciplined. I want it to be like hanging with a good friend who I can hear from."

And so those three words, "I love you," eventually, over much time, became sentences; then sentences became paragraphs; and that half-hour became four hours; and those three words became sixty pages of hearing from the King of kings and the Lord of lords. That's cool!

Now, lots of people think there's something special about being a pastor. Many put pastors on a different plane of existence. Stop it! And if you only knew! A lot of people, when I share stories, are like, "Oh yeah, that's fine for you." No. What I'm talking about, hearing the voice of the Lord, isn't just for bald pastors. It's for all people who have a pulse.

The Lord wants to speak to you like he speaks to me. And he wants to tell you he loves you, and he wants to tell you words of affirmation. He wants to bring you words of direction, words of clarity; sometimes words of correction, because you're going to need it. There's too much at stake for us to go through our Christian walk and treat it like Christian voodoo. But the deal is that it's up to you to do anything about it. This training of the ears, it's *training*. It takes effort, time, space. But I'm telling you there's too much freedom at stake for you to not go through it. When God speaks, and we as individuals hear God speak, amazing things happen on the inside. And it's not just for our benefit. When we hear the voice of the Lord, lost people who are headed toward death will be found and find life.

Will you put in the time to train your inner ear? Will you train yourself to hear God speak? Will you set aside time to spend in solitude, listening? Will you let the Lord bless you, transform you, and use you?

That's your homework. Listen.

Prayer

Lord, we acknowledge that many of us have grown up in a tradition apart from the Holy Spirit. Lord, we set that aside and embrace the truth of the Scriptures. We declare we are your disciples. Therefore we declare we want your spirit. Spirit of God, come and move. Come and transform us. Spirit of God, come and sanctify this ground. Make this a holy place, Lord. Holy Spirit, remove the distractions of life, that we might be fully present. Lord, we ask that your spirit would help us to be still. Still, Lord, so that we might commune with you. Amen.

Go Deeper

→ Take twenty minutes a day this week to listen for the voice of the Lord.

Chapter 13
Naked

Nudity is wonderful. Naked is good.

Let's go back to the very basics of why Jesus came. The whole reason we do church. It's because we were here and God was way over there and the whole reason Jesus came was to bring us together with God, to bring us into relationship with God.

So how can we walk into more of the freedom that our relationship with God offers us?

One way is by realizing that naked is good. We know this as children. Have you ever seen a kid just doff the diaper and run around the house buck naked? Kids know intuitively that naked is good. There's something free and refreshing about being out of the confines of clothing. But something happens when we get a little older. We get inhibited. More nervous and more shy. So much so that just hearing the word "nude" or "naked" in public makes us giggle nervously.

Nakedness is God's idea. In Genesis 2:25 we read, talking of Adam and Eve: "Adam and his wife were both naked, and they felt no shame." Genesis is the first book of the Old Testament. It was given to Hebrew people, so originally it was written in the Hebrew language. Now the Hebrew people have a culture that encourages them to look more deeply into things than we do in North America. We read "they were naked and they felt no shame" and we just take that statement at face value— they were naked and they felt no shame. But Hebrew people would read that Adam and Eve were naked and felt no shame and think, Oh, there's something more than physical nakedness going on here. "They were naked" implies they were emotionally vulnerable, spiritually revealed; there was no hiding any part of their being.

Actual physical nakedness is only a small part of the meaning of the word "naked" in the Genesis context. Hebrew people reading Genesis in Hebrew would understand that the text is telling us that Adam and Eve were fully seen, and there was no shame in them. Naked is good.

I don't want anyone to run out in the street buck naked. You'd get arrested. When I say naked is good, I'm using the word naked in its deeper Hebrew sense. Emotional and spiritual nakedness means you're fully seen and known, and it's good. It's very freeing to be naked, figuratively, and to feel no shame.

But after Genesis, chapter 2, comes what? Chapter 3. And you know about Adam and Eve; they bit that apple, they walked in disobedience, they said no to God. We want our own way. And the moment they turned from God, they saw themselves as they truly were, and they were embarrassed about their nakedness. What did they do? They made garments out of fig leaves. And they hid, because having walked away from the Lord, they now thought that their true selves were no longer good enough to be with God. They had to hide and cover themselves, because they didn't want to be seen as they really were.

Humanity has been "fig leafin'" ever since. I mean, think about the way we hide behind our own fig leaves. We're afraid that if we are truly seen for who we are it won't be good enough, so we hide and we pose and we pretend. We fig leaf all through life.

Bald men like me are some of the biggest fig leafers in the world. Back in my dad's generation, what did men do to hide baldness? The comb-over, right? Or if you're like my Uncle Don, you'd have the comb-forward. And these comb-over and comb-forward people feared wind. Because if the wind blew, they would be revealed, their secret would be out, their fig leaf would be removed, and it would be awful. Because who they really were was not good enough.

When my friend Mike was getting married way back when, we were sitting around the rehearsal dinner table with him and his brother-in-law, and this dude had no hair, like twelve pieces on top of his head. I had about fifteen, so I had just a few more than him, but I made this comment during dinner: "Hey dude, us bald people need to stick together." And do you know what? It ruined the whole wedding for him because I had outed him and revealed to the world what he hoped people weren't noticing, that he was a bald man. The real him was embarrassing, something that shouldn't be talked about.

I, on the other hand, just shave my head because I want to pretend that I chose baldness. It's another form of hiding. You think I'm actually tough and cool and I choose baldness, when in reality I'm hiding. We, like Adam and Eve, are fearful that when people see us for who we really are, we won't be likeable. So we pose.

When I was a little boy, in fourth grade, my dad and I were at a boat show in Michigan's Upper Peninsula, where he was stationed as an air force guy, and we went into a bathroom together. My elementary school had these really cool sinks where you stepped on a pedal at the base of the sink and the water came out. So we go to the restroom and, I'm trying to be delicate here, Dad thought the sink was something it wasn't. And I'm like, "Dad, that's not what that's for." And he said, "Yes it is. It's a urinal." I'm like, "No, it isn't." "Yes it is." "No, it isn't, Dad." And I stepped on the pedal. "Dad, that's a sink." "It's not a sink." So, hmmm...speaking delicately, Dad took care of business in the sink. "A guy is over there washing his hands, Dad. That is a sink." "It's not a sink."

He couldn't handle being seen having made a mistake. So he hid behind denial. Believe me, it was not a sink.

But I'm my father's son. I used to work out on a bench press machine. The last thing I would do before I got up was increase the weight so the next person would sit down and think, Wow, that guy is kind of scrawny but he's stronger than he looks. Because the real me isn't good enough. Maybe you are a man who is totally un-mechanical, and you go to get your oil changed and a manly man covered with grease from head to toe asks, "You want 10W30 or 5W30?" You don't have a clue and inside you're thinking, "Oh crap, just please don't touch me, you're dirty." But on the outside you're reaching out to shake the guy's hand. The real us might not be the better us. So we hide.

If you're a woman, do you feel more comfortable around men than women? Maybe other women are competition and you tend to compare yourself with them. Are you woman enough to be around other women?

The real us isn't good enough, so we hide behind our fig leaves. Sometimes our personality is a fig leaf. We realized at a young age that a certain type of personality will gain us acceptance. Maybe you're the funny one. Everywhere you go people are laughing. God did make you funny, but you've overdone it and your personality has become your survival technique. Now you always have to be funny. Sometimes you have to hide what you really feel.

Or maybe you're the mellow guy. Nothing gets to you. *I'm just laid back. I'm just chill. Nothing bothers me.* Now there might be some truth in that. Some people are more laid back. But this persona that nothing bothers you can also be a fig leaf to hide behind. Or maybe you're like, oh, he's the smart one or she's the smart one. The fashionable one. The athletic one. Good with cars. We take these things that God has given us and we concoct a huge fig leaf known as our personality. And like Adam and Eve we go into hiding, and we're fearful that the wind will come and blow our fig leaf away.

The problem with fig leaves, though, is that they're deadly. They will kill us. See, back in the garden, God's purpose for Adam and Eve was this: to be chillin' with him. Just to hang out, and for him to talk to us. For us to hear him. For us to be tight with the Lord as a friend. Jesus says, "I no longer call you servants, I call you friends." But when we put on our fig leaves we say to friendship with the Lord: "Get away. Stay over there." And when we hide behind fig leaves we take the grace of Jesus, which is for every knucklehead sinner that's ever lived, and we say, "Well, it's kinda good for me, but not really. I'm hiding. Stay away." Our fig leaves keep us from the deep and rich communion with almighty God that he desires for us.

I've said many times, if you want to be a better husband, better father, better wife, better mother, better son, better daughter, better student, better employer, better neighbor, don't worry about working on any of that. Just get tight with Jesus, and those things will fall into place. Our fig leaves keep us from being the people that God intends us to be. Our fig leaves keep us from getting tight with the Lord.

And as we see all through Genesis and beyond, our fig leaves are a sledgehammer in the enemy's hand. The enemy is the prince of the kingdom of darkness, Satan, Lucifer. He uses our fig leaves as a source of shame, and he begins to whisper, "You're an idiot, a loser, an addict. You're no good. God can't love you. How will anyone ever love you? How are they even going to like you?" And because we're so scared that people will find out about our stupid past, Satan beats us over the head with it. It becomes a sledgehammer that beats us silly, and we walk around defeated and broken because Satan is using what we've hidden in the closet to beat us up.

How many of you have thought you were an idiot, a loser, a bonehead who's never going to get any better? How many of you have been ashamed of your past?

Our fig leaves also kill those around us. Here's what I learned at church as a little kid. I knew that I had issues. I had a pulse, so therefore, what? I had issues. You got a pulse, you got issues. Yet I learned that no one else did. I was aware that I was a little off from time to time, but I went to church and saw the preacher and all the people talking about how great life is. God is great. God is good. Never had a bad day in my entire life. Yeah! Amen! How are you today? FINE! By golly, I was the only one who had bad days!

Now that may be true a lot of the time, but every day, *forever?* So I learned as little kid that the only one who had any issues in church was me. I was the only messed up little guy. I mean, my pastor certainly had everything together. He never once mentioned that he had any struggles. Leaders of the church? Adults? Oh, no. Everybody was fine. And so I realized that in order for me to fit in the church community, I needed to have some fig leaves to hide behind. When people came up to me and asked, "How are you doing?"—what did I tell them? "Fine." But all the while I was dying inside.

Remember the story about my friend Jamie asking me about my parents' divorce? I told him I was fine, even though I wasn't remotely fine. I told him that because I was scared to death to let people see the brokenness inside of me. Because I was afraid they wouldn't accept the real me.

When we live behind our fig leaves, it tells others they had better stay behind theirs too. Jesus said in Luke, chapter 4, "[The Spirit of the Lord] has sent me to proclaim freedom for the prisoners." Fig leaves are not worn by people who are free. And when we stay behind our fig leaves, we keep other people in shackles too.

If we choose to forgo our fig leaves and say, "Here I am," others will begin scratching their heads and some of them will be like, "Wow, that dude's really messed up. I can relate to him. That dude is messed up, but I've seen the Lord do something in his life. Maybe God can do something in my life." When we get rid of our fig leaves, many people will find freedom from theirs and walk into the purpose that God made them for.

But not everyone will clap with joy, will they? A father and son from the congregation I serve were over at another church one week. The son was leading worship and then they both shared some of their story and the dad, just briefly, talked about some of his pain from being brought up in an environment where there wasn't a lot of affection. He didn't say much about it, just a little bit. And then he went on to describe how that can impact you when you're young. He went on to talk about how the Lord set him free and made him a new man. He was just naked in front of the people at church that day. Many loved it. Wow, refreshing. But the pastor got some phone calls and letters from people who didn't like the "nudity" that the father had exhibited. It made them uncomfortable—and God forbid this should happen at church!

When we get naked, when we get raw and honest and reveal ourselves, it's going to make some people uncomfortable and they're going to say, "Get behind your fig leaf." Brothers and sisters, if you want freedom, say no. Naked is good.

You will never hear me say life is always great. I have struggled with depression. I was addicted to pornography. When I was in third grade I saw my first hit of pornography, and by fifth grade I was addicted. Now I'm free. My past is not in the closet anymore, but for years those things were. I was hiding and I was in bondage.

Basically every guy has struggled with pornography in one way or another. If a guy says he hasn't, he's probably lying. (I know a few men who have never struggled with this, but only a few.) I remember when I led a campus group at a nearby university. I would get up in front of these guys and say, "Guys, you gotta stop. You gotta stop it." How many guys do you think found freedom when I did that? None. But when I got up and said, "Hey fellas, here's my struggle. When I was in third grade..." How many guys found freedom when I revealed myself? A lot.

Adam and Eve were naked and they felt no shame. We're all a bunch of messed up suckers. But praise God for Jesus. We don't need to pretend we don't have issues, because the Lord came to take care of our fig leaves and the need to hide behind them.

So, will you live nakedly? When somebody asks you how you are doing and you're not doing fine, will you please not say, "Fine"? You don't have to give all the details, but if someone asks how you're doing and you're not doing good, you can say, "You know, I'm not doing too good, but I'll be better tomorrow." That's probably true. Refuse to hide. You'll find freedom. You'll find intimacy, and the people around you will be freer too.

Nudity is wonderful. Naked is good.

Prayer

Lord, pull us into your presence. Usher us into the throne room. Lord, thank you for the gift of worship. We want to encounter the living God, the King of kings and Lord of lords. Lord, we want to encounter you. We want to be led by you, Lord. We need your presence in order to worship. We need your presence in order to grow. We need your presence, heavenly Father. Send your spirit in force today. Amen.

Go Deeper

→ On a scale of one to ten, how scared are you at the thought of living life "naked"? Why?

→ What "fig leaves" have you been wearing?

Chapter 14
Iron

The notion of teamwork is God's idea. As it says in the ancient Scriptures, in the book of Ecclesiastes, "Two are better than one."

The verse we're going to hang our hat on is Proverbs 27:17: "As iron sharpens iron, so one man sharpens another"...or one woman sharpens another.

Maybe you find this thought annoying, because the sound of iron on iron is a nasty noise, creepy. Imagine the sound of two iron knives scraping together. It might make you cringe. But it gets at a really important biblical truth: none of us was created to live life alone.

At the very beginning of time, one person was living in the garden, in Paradise, by himself. He was alone, and God said: This is not good. You need another. "Two are better than one."

David, before he was king of Israel, was closer than a brother with his friend Jonathan, and together the two of them did great things.

When Saul stopped persecuting Christians and became the apostle Paul, he had his buddy Barnabas, and the two of them together did wonderful things.

When Jesus sent his disciples out to do ministry he always sent them in pairs, because Jesus knew that two are better than one, that iron sharpens iron. Jesus had communion with the Father like no one else. Yet when Jesus began his ministry, he gathered the twelve disciples and walked in communion with them. Not only so that they might change the world, but also so that they might learn this truth: men and women sharpen each other as iron sharpens iron.

The poet John Donne said it this way: "No man is an island." No one stands alone. Batman has Robin, Tom has Jerry, Mutt has Jeff. Even super heroes don't go it alone. Even popular culture says there needs to be teamwork.

In the Garden of Eden, Adam and Eve experienced a rift in their relationship because of Satan, the father of the kingdom of darkness, the father of lies, the accuser of the brethren, the stealer of life, the giver of death. As John 10:10 says, "The thief comes only to steal and kill and destroy." Satan wants to destroy every one of God's creations, which happens to be all of us. And one of the ways he does this is by bringing about isolation, by dividing us from each other.

In the beginning we see Adam and Eve in conflict. She bites the apple; she blames him, he blames her; they are in broken community. As much as we all long for community, the reality of it freaks us out. Just like the noise of iron on iron, at times actually living in close, intimate, open, raw, honest, fully seen, faults-and-all community will bug the snot out of you. But the powerful flip-side—when community is deep and rich—is that you also will be fully loved in community and fully accepted. And the kingdom of darkness wants none of that.

I'm thinking of my good friend Mike. Back in 1993 I entered seminary, having graduated from the fine institution of higher education known as Ferris State University. I entered a three-year masters program, and I was spending six hours a day studying Greek when I met this dude named Mike. We connected instantly. We used to laugh and have all kinds of fun, and after six hours of class work he and I would go to the library together. Working together we would get our Greek homework done in two or three hours, while others, working alone, needed six hours...ugh. Two is better than one. Iron sharpens iron. He and I made one another better Greek students. Not only did we help each other academically, we began to pray together, laugh together, and share our deepest fears and dreams.

At the end of that summer Greek class, Mike was the top student in our class. I was number two, and he still rubs it in to this day. Two are better than one. We connected so deeply and had so much fun that we decided we would take every single class together for the next three years.

And we did. And we had a lot of fun. The seminary made Mike the morning janitor. He had to empty the garbage cans, so they gave him a key to the building. We wreaked a little good natured havoc on that place together. When Professor Brown became our preaching prof, his office got painted brown. And maybe a little passive-aggressively, when another staff member was bugging us, we broke into his office with five rolls of yarn and spider-webbed his whole office. He couldn't even walk in. Iron sharpens iron!

And yet, even though in our hearts we long to be part of a team, even though the importance of relationships is shown all through Scripture and our culture, the kingdom of darkness has been set against this happening from the beginning of time.

Every moment of seminary, we walked together, and it was like God meant it to be, David and Jonathan, laughing and connecting on deep (and very shallow) levels. But the thing is, we experienced that when the world, the culture, saw this, the reaction was sometimes, Please stop it; there's something wrong with that. Just like people sometimes cringe when they hear iron scraping on iron.

Kristy (my girlfriend then, now my wife) and I would go down to Indiana for Thanksgiving and bring Mike along. We'd hang out with my family and do the Thanksgiving thing together. And Mike met my Uncle Morris, a great guy. My Uncle Morris is gay. He has lived a gay lifestyle since he was in high school. When he saw the closeness between Mike and me, he could only comprehend one thing. He pulled my mom aside and said, "Judy, I'm concerned for Rob and Kristy, because Mike is a gay man madly in love with Rob and it's going to mess them all up."

My uncle had good intentions, but sadly no paradigm or model for understanding a close relationship between men other than that they must be gay. Then again, when Mike teases me about being the second best Greek student, I have something to tease him about every now and then too...thank you, Uncle Morris.

It wasn't just my Uncle Morris who didn't get the friendship I had with Mike. Some people at the seminary didn't get it either.

In seminary you spend three years of your life studying ancient languages, Bible, theology, and a lot of other things. It can be awful. But Mike and I finished it, and because we were together we actually had a lot of fun in seminary.

We graduated in May 1996, but in February of '96 we'd been called into the office of the dean of students. He said, "Hey, you guys, we've watched you and we've had several formal complaints in writing. We believe the reason you've taken every class together over the past three years was so you could cheat together. We want you to bring in every assignment and every test you've taken in the past three years."

We went home and we dug out our files, and fortunately we had saved everything. We each brought a huge stack of papers and plopped it on this poor sucker's desk, and he had to spend all weekend going through our assignments. Only to discover that they were incredibly different. Our work was not even remotely similar. The reality was that even at the seminary they had nowhere to fit in the close relationship Mike and I shared. Because like the sound of iron sharpening iron, it could be bothersome and strange and uncomfortable.

We understand the need for friendship, we even long for it. We want it, but we don't want it too close, because it's a little scary, daunting. Sometimes it sounds like iron sharpening iron. We love being together, but often we keep it at the level of talking about sports or going shopping. But that's not the level of relationship the Scriptures talk about. See, the Lord has a plan for each of us, and it's a plan of peace and joy and fulfillment. It's a plan with purpose and significance. It's a plan that includes who you already are but that allows you to express yourself more freely and more like Jesus.

You will never reach the best you can be without being in relationship with others who want the same thing. Without even knowing it, some of us have been dying for this.

But there is a thief who steals, kills, and destroys, and when we walk alone we are vulnerable to his lies. That's what happened to King David. When he was with his friend Jonathan, things were good. David walked with the Lord as he was walking with Jonathan, and they were doing great and mighty things. But when David became king of Israel, he began to live in isolation, and he began to do stupid things. Does that sound like anyone's story other than mine? Because when you're alone, you don't have someone to say, "Dude, you're being a knucklehead." What others would recognize as a bad idea, we think, Huh, that sounds like a good idea to me. And so David made a bad decision. In 2 Samuel 11:1 it says:

> In the spring, at the time when kings go off to war, David sent Joab out with the king's men and the whole Israelite army. They destroyed the Ammonites and besieged Rabbah. But David remained in Jerusalem.

Joab and the army went off and David let them go and stayed home alone. One day he gets up on the rooftop to take an afternoon nap and sees a beautiful woman who's naked, taking a bath. And he has what he thinks is a good idea: Hey, I'm king. I can get what I want. I'll have a servant bring her up to my room and I will have my way with her. Good idea.

Had Jonathan been on the scene, he would have said, "Yo, David, you're being stupid! What are you thinking? She's a married woman. You're a king. You can't do that. You're a child of the Lord, a man after God's own heart. You cannot do that."

But David was alone. He seduced her; he had his way with her. How could she say no to the most powerful man in the world? She got pregnant by David, and David had another great idea: I'll cover this one up. So he ended up having her husband killed. It's a great idea. No one will ever know. I'll just get rid of the husband.

What a great idea, right? Yes, great idea. David—you're an idiot! Don't do this! But he was alone. So he had her husband killed, which brought on all kinds of pain and brokenness.

Friends, the stakes are too high to go it alone.

A good friend of mine, a therapist, helped set me free with some great godly therapy back when I was more messed up than I am today. He has set many people I know free. He was a tool of the Lord, without question.

A few of us began to join with him in friendships that went beyond counseling. We were in relationships that allowed us to stay on the surface or go deep. As we walked this way with him, we came to realize that for a decade or more he had been doing life alone. He likened himself to Zorro. A therapeutic Zorro. That's what he called himself, and in many ways it was an accurate description. Above his office door hung a sword and mask like the ones Zorro wears in old TV shows and the movies.

In a way it was awesome that this guy was like Zorro, because Zorro set people free, right? Zorro is a hero. Unfortunately, also like Zorro, this dude worked alone. And about ten years before we had come on the scene, like David, he thought he had a good idea about how to minister to a female client. And he acted on this idea, which was in reality a really bad idea. As a result, he lost his practice and hit unbelievable roadblocks in his marriage. His was removed from ministry and eventually spent six weeks in jail. Because he was malicious and evil? No. Because he was human and alone. One of the most tragic parts of this story is that I firmly believe if he had understood the importance of community all those years ago, he would still be practicing and setting people free today.

Friends, the stakes are too high for you not to live in community. But be aware that living in community is going to take effort. When I realized I needed to connect with more people, I called some of my friends and said, "Hey let's meet, and let's take it deeper." All of the fellas in that group had to find the time to make it happen, and someone had to begin revealing the junk in his life. And I think I speak for all of us when I say that we are better and freer people because we are in community.

But it's not just guy groups. Kristy and I have what we call a band of couples, a few couples that meet regularly. We sharpen and challenge each other and help each other laugh. This is what I believe the Scriptures are speaking about when they say two are better than one for they have a good return for their work. This is what the Lord is talking about in Proverbs when it says "as iron sharpens iron so one man [or one woman] sharpens another." It's what we all need. The world will be a better place when you put the effort into living in community.

As iron sharpens iron, so one man sharpens another. As iron sharpens iron, so one woman sharpens another.

Prayer

I need you, Lord. I need you to minister to me, Lord. I declare by faith that you are good. I declare by faith, Lord, that you have my best interest at heart and I believe, by faith, that you have abundance for me, that you have joy for me, that you have peace for me. I declare by faith, Lord, that you have purpose and significance and meaning for me. That you have community and family and laughter for me. I declare by faith, Lord, that you have restoration for me and healing for me and freedom for me. And

I declare by faith, Lord, that you have victory for me in the name of Jesus. Amen.

Go Deeper

→ Who are the people who are serving as "iron" in your life?

→ How might you take your friendships to a more "sharpening" level?

Chapter 15
Solitude

Earlier, I busted out some facts on voodoo and laid out the fact that this thing called Christianity has nothing to do with doing a, b, or c to get a, b, or c. The entire point of what we're about is for you and Jesus to be tight together.

We've also looked at being naked, figuratively, and that naked is good. And we've looked at the importance of community—that for you to be tight with Jesus, one way to help you down that path is for you to get in community. We talked about how you were created to be in community, how you need it to grow as a disciple of Jesus, and why church can't substitute for community. The church I pastor is a great gathering of people. But I also need a smaller group of people to just do life with. If you don't have that group, your relationship with the Lord will just begin to dry up. You need to get plugged into a community. Community. People. You need it.

But now I want to talk about this thing called solitude. I want to tell you that you need to go be alone. You're probably thinking, so which is it? Community or solitude?

Do you like community? Do you like solitude? Which do you like better, chocolate or vanilla? How about college athletics or professional athletics? Burgers or pizza? A good novel or a good movie?

Let me tell you something about the word "or." It's evil. "Or" is evil. Repeat after me: "Or" is evil. "And" is my friend.

Why chocolate or vanilla? Why not both? Why not chocolate *and* vanilla? In fact, when they're together they're better. Why college or pro? Why not both? Why not burgers *and* pizza? Why not a good novel *and* a good movie? Why not community and solitude?

"Or" is evil. We need to embrace the beauty of "and." We need "both" and "and." We saw that Jesus taught his disciples the importance of community; now we'll see that Jesus taught them how important it is to be alone too. If you're not in community *and* spending time alone with the Father, you're going to die spiritually. We need to be people of solitude, too.

Without solitude your relationship with the Lord will become dry and crusty and forgotten, and eventually null and void. I'm using strong language on purpose. You need solitude, but don't take my word for it; take the Word's word for it. Here's a boatload of Bible verses, starting with Mathew 14:23 (NRSV):

> "After [Jesus] had dismissed the crowds, he went up the mountain by himself to pray."

> "In the morning, while it was still very dark, [Jesus] got up and went out to a deserted place, and there he prayed" (Mark 1:35, NRSV).

> "Come with me [Jesus] by yourselves to a quiet place and get some rest" (Mark 6:31).

> "At daybreak [Jesus] departed and went into a deserted place" (Luke 4:42, NRSV).

> "[Jesus] withdrew from [the disciples] about a stone's throw, knelt down, and prayed" (Luke 22:41).

> "Be still before the Lord, and wait patiently for him" (Psalm 37:7, NRSV).

> "Now then, stand still and see this great thing the Lord is about to do before your eyes!" (1 Samuel 12:16, NRSV).

> "The Lord will fight for you, you have only to keep still" (Exodus 14:14, NRSV).

To grow in our walk with the Lord, we absolutely need to be with each other and we absolutely need to leave each other. The Scriptures are clear but so are some old dead people who were wise. Charles Haddon Spurgeon, a British preacher who lived from 1834 to 1892, said, "I commend solitude to any of you who are seeking salvation. First, that you may study well your case as in the sight of God. Few men [or women] truly know themselves as they really are."

"Settle yourselves," says another old dead person, Teresa of Avila, who was born five hundred years ago. "Settle yourself in solitude and you will come upon Him in yourself." She's saying that when you're alone and quiet you will find God.

Yet another old dead guy, Austin Phelps (American Congregational minister, 1820-1890), said:

> It has been said that no great work in literature or in science was ever wrought by a man who did not love solitude. We may lay it down as an elemental principle of religion, that no large growth in holiness was ever gained by one who did not take time to be often and long alone with God.

If you want to grow you gotta be alone.

What am I talking about? Solitude. Being alone. It's referred to throughout Scripture. A bunch of smart old dead people recommend it. And at first glance there's something kind of romantic about being alone. Tranquility. Ahhh, solitude. Yes.

When I first brushed up against this concept of needing to be alone, I thought of Henry David Thoreau on Walden Pond. "I'm going to get alone and I'm going to do great things." I saw that Jesus got up very early in the morning to be alone and commune with God, and I said, "Wow. Solitude. Yes."

You might be thinking, hmm...the notion of solitude sounds kind of appealing. I'll be like Henry David Thoreau. I'm going to go where it's quiet and write poetry and I'm going to watch birds and have a nice tranquil, peaceful time. It's going to be very nice. Solitude.

That's what I thought, until I tried some solitude. And after having tried solitude, my thoughts went from Ahh...tranquility... to Oh, this sucks. It about killed me.

The first time I spent a large chunk of time alone was when I went backpacking on Isle Royale with my dad and my brother. Isle Royale is a pristine island wilderness in northwest Lake Superior. For four days the three of us hiked the island. We saw a bunch of moose; it was awesome. And then my dad and brother left, and for six days I was entirely alone. And I was going to write poetry. And I was going to have a really nice, tranquil time. So I'd walk a few miles and sit down to watch the moose play, and I said to myself, Ahhh. Solitude. But that was only the first half-hour.

The second hour came around and already I was beginning to think, Dang, I'm bored. The third hour rolled around and I thought, Man, I'm kind of lonely. By the fourth hour I was thinking, Well, I'll just go to bed. And it was like five o'clock. I'm not kidding you. By day six, I was insane. Have you ever been alone with yourself for a long period of time?

You see, when you're with people—and you need to be with people—your focus is mostly outside yourself; you don't have to look inside all that much. But when you're alone, away from the distractions of the world, it can make you nuts. And you'll note that in the Bible it says that the disciples withdrew to be with Jesus. They didn't withdraw to be with a movie, or TV, or a novel. See, if you give me a novel, I can be alone for hours, days. In fact the thought of being by myself with a good book and no kids climbing on me and screaming or fighting with each other, that sounds like heaven. But when I was alone, without any distractions, just me and God, I literally about went insane. And I thought, Man, I'm evil. Because when I was alone and looked inside, I saw all the things I could cover everywhere else, and I said, "Oh my."

I was two years into my seminary training, and at the end of my six days alone on the island I said, "I'm done. I'm quitting. I can't be a pastor; I'm an idiot." Fortunately God said, "Yep, you are an idiot, and I use idiots. And now that you've seen yourself, I can begin to use you." It was awful. Just awful. Friends, solitude is not something peaceful and tranquil. It's incredibly difficult.

Another old dead guy named St. Anthony, who was known as the father of monks, called solitude "the terrible trial." It is painful. But it hurts good. To be alone is incredibly painful, and to be alone is exactly what we need. In the past when I've needed solitude, I've spent time with the monks at St. Gregory's Abbey in Three Rivers. I've talked with friends of mine about my experiences there, and they get really excited. A few of them have gone with me to the monastery over the years. I would say, "Now, we're going to be there all day. You cool with that?" "Oh yeah," my friend would say, "I'm good with that." Sometimes literally a half-hour after arriving at the monastery, my friend would have to leave. Squirminess had set in.

I want to make sure you get this. If we miss the charge to be alone, we're going to miss the opportunity for the Lord to grow us. To be alone with ourselves is scary, but it is good. To be alone and naked with yourself is incredibly difficult, but when you get naked with yourself, figuratively speaking, that's when the Lord begins to change you. You will be transformed. You will find more freedom, and you will find more of God when you're alone. It's very difficult, and the kingdom of darkness is going to do everything it can to keep you from doing it. God's Word teaches us that we don't go through life unopposed. The kingdom of darkness is set against us and works hard to keep us from doing this thing called solitude.

A pastor friend of mine went to his elder board and said, "I want to spend every morning from eight to nine at home in my study to be alone with the Lord." And the elders of this church looked him in the face and said, "We don't pay you to be alone with the Lord. We pay you to do ministry. No, you're not going to do that."

It's been said that if the devil can't make you bad, he'll make you busy. Busyness can be as bad as being bad. We need to take time out. Slow down. When we allow ourselves, the culture, and the kingdom of darkness to keep us with people and on the go all the time, we literally go through life without rest and without connection to the Father. The world screams, "Don't just sit there, do something!" The Word of God says, "Don't just do something, sit there." Solitude.

Now, what I don't want to do is give you another duty that you must do. Instead I want to awaken a hunger in you for solitude. I have been a man of solitude and I have also been a man of no solitude, and when I take time to walk in solitude I'm a better man. I am more peaceful, freer, more relaxed, more disciplined. When I'm a man of no solitude I'm more uptight, more edgy, touchier, more likely to get angry at the driver who cuts me off. When we walk in solitude there's a goodness that comes from being alone with God. Solitude.

On the other hand, it's important to plan solitude. It's not going to just happen. Plan for it. Put it on the calendar; mark the date. Plan it. Where are you going to go? The monks in Three Rivers would love to host you for a day. Maybe go to a park, the beach, the woods, a tree stand—wherever you would love to be alone for an hour. Choose a day and a place, and plan what you are going to do. You need to plan, and you need to take a journal and a pen. How many of you are easily distracted like me? Bring a pen and a piece of paper and write down your thoughts and your prayers. Bring your Bible, maybe a devotional, and your latest Brian Fraaza worship CD, and worship the Lord. Be ready for an adjustment time when you're thinking, This is awful. Be ready for distractions.

But also be ready to be transformed. Solitude.

Prayer

Lord, we pray that your spirit would come and bring peace; in addition to joy, we need peace. The peace that the apostle Paul talks about in Philippians 4:7, where it says, "The peace of God, which surpasses all understanding, will guard your hearts and your minds."

We pray against the wiles of Satan, who brings discouragement, and despair, and anxiety, Lord, and we declare peace here today in the name of Jesus.

Go Deeper

→ Does the thought of spending a day alone with no TV, books, people, etc. sound good to you? Why or why not?

→ When was the last time you spent a large chunk of time alone? What was it like for you?

→ Go be alone for a couple hours this week.

Chapter 16
Others

The whole point of the cross and everything else related to Jesus could probably be summed up in the word "freedom." The apostle Paul says in 2 Corinthians, "Where the spirit of the Lord is, there is freedom." The same apostle, in Galatians, chapter 5, makes a wonderfully redundant statement: "For freedom Christ has set us free." In Luke, chapter 4, Jesus, quoting Isaiah, says that he has come to set the prisoners free.

Following Jesus is all about freedom, and that's good news for anyone who has ever been shackled or bound by anything in life.

Just in case you think that doesn't include you, let me remind you, you have a pulse, and therefore you have issues. Whether you are young or old, somewhere, somehow, life has tried to bind you and shackle you. The good news of Jesus is that he came to set us free. Did I say good news? It's great news!

I remember as a kid feeling motivated to become a preacher because the preachers I grew up under proclaimed this great news that Jesus came to set you free. He came to heal you, to release you. Yes! What a great message! But these preachers were so boring in their presentation of this exciting message that they would quickly put everybody to sleep. I wondered if they actually believed what they were saying. How many of you, when you were little, could tell someone the number of tiles on the church ceiling? How many of you doodled on the friendship pads while the pastor was preaching?

Honestly, part of my call to be a preacher was to tell the exciting and good news of freedom in Jesus without boring everybody to death! At an early age, I couldn't articulate it, but as I grew older I recognized I would work as hard as I could to make it hard for others not to listen to the good news: Jesus sets us free! My job would be to make it hard for people not to hear the word of God. So if I just simply got in front of a congregation and read notes...blah, blah, blah...I would not be doing what God called me to do. I would not be fulfilling my purpose and my calling. My job is to make it hard for people not to hear the good news of Jesus. So I was thinking about the lengths I've gone to to engage people so that they can hear the good news.

I remembered preaching at my grandma's church when I was nineteen. I was doing a lesson on Christmas; you know, about Jesus being born in a stable, and the beauty of God; the King of kings and Lord of lords taking on the form of a baby born in a stable. So I went to my great grandma's farm to get cow manure for the service. People were engaged.

I also remembered when, early in The River's life as a Christ-centered community, over at our Lake Street building, I brought a basketball up front to illustrate some point I was making. Somebody in the back of the room was like, "Throw it here." What happened next was awful. Thinking, hey, audience participation is good, I threw the basketball as hard as I could toward the back. A first-time visitor sitting with her head down looked up to see a basketball flying toward her face. I instantly thought, oh my. I'm done. I'm going to be a shoe salesman. But praise the Lord, a regular attender stood up behind her, reached forward, and caught the ball inches before it hit her in the face. It was one of the dumbest things I've ever done.

Another time I wanted to teach on father Abraham and the Lord entering into Abram's life and calling out the blessings and promises to come. I was dressed in an old robe to look like Abraham. It was going to be a serious drama-type thing, and I knew I was in trouble the moment I stepped out, because everyone in whole place started to laugh at me.

One Sunday, to make a point about the importance of play, we played P.I.G. while I taught. We had the hoop out on the floor, and we were shooting and playing basketball while I was trying to teach that play is a biblical concept and that it's part of our road to freedom to incorporate play in our lives.

All of this to get to this story: I once showed some nasty pictures of feet on the big screen at church. I was preparing to teach on the passage "How beautiful are the feet of those who bring good news!" (Romans 10:15). Jake, my oldest son, Wil, our executive pastor, and I were in my office the Friday before I was going to teach on the passage, and just for fun we Google-imaged "nasty feet." That Sunday I learned that if the tool of engagement is too over the top, it can take over the whole teaching and you forget the point you wanted to make. All that I remember, probably along with everyone else who was there, are those nasty feet that I showed on screen.

For some reason as I was writing this I kept coming back to those nasty feet images. To be sure we need the feet God gave us, probably so we don't fall over when we walk. But it is undeniable that feet can be gross. I've learned better than to show nasty feet images, yet there is a powerful point in those images connected to the fact that Jesus washed his disciples' feet. People who lived in the Old and New Testament eras certainly would agree. Most people didn't get pedicures back then. They didn't get pedicures and they rarely had roads or sidewalks of any kind. They walked in dust and dirt and mud, and they didn't wear sneakers or boots. What did they have to wear? Sandals. So I'm sure Old and New Testament folks would agree that feet can be nasty. And yet the Lord of lords washed feet.

When people entered a house, a synagogue, or a building of any kind their feet would be dusty, nasty, and dirty. So what did they do? They had servants whose sole job was to wash feet. Sign me up for that job! My goodness, punch me in the nose instead. Some poor sucker had the awful job of washing those nasty old feet. Who would want that job? Yuck. It was a low-end-of-the-totem-pole kinda job. If you were the lowest servant, you washed feet.

When Jesus and his disciples shared their last meal together before he was arrested, before they sat down to eat, Jesus poured water into a basin and began to wash his disciples' nasty, dirty, stinky feet and dry them with a towel that he had wrapped around him. Jesus. Not the lowest of the house servants. Jesus. The Son of God. God taking on flesh. The King of kings, the Lord of lords. He poured water and he washed their feet. Is he stupid? Is he nuts? Didn't Jesus know the Jewish theology of the day—that God was not going to come and serve, he was the one who would be served? Jewish folks couldn't get their heads around the idea that God would wash anyone's feet. You would wash his feet and serve him, not vice versa.

It wasn't just the Hebrew people who knew what Jesus obviously didn't. It was the Greek people too. Jesus lived in a Greek world. Greek mythology, their way of thinking about the spirit world, taught that the gods were very capricious and fickle (kinda like us). In order to keep the gods from snapping and flying off the handle and punishing you, if you were Greek and you believed in Greek mythology, you had to serve the gods. Try Googling the list of sacrifices and offerings that Greek people had to make to appease the gods. It's a long, long list, because the gods were meant to be served, and certainly would never serve humans. Jesus clearly didn't get the memo.

And it's clear that he doesn't know what we certainly know. People in our world who have power and position and influence are the people we serve. When LeBron James was deciding where to play he could have asked for just about anything in the world. People wined and dined him and offered him money beyond his wildest dreams. It's inconceivable that anyone would have gone to LeBron as he was deciding where to play and said, "Hey, will you wash our feet? Would you serve us? Come to our city and just serve us." I mean, in our culture we clearly get what Jesus didn't. Those in power and position, they're the ones to be served, right?

How many of you have been to a church with signs at the best parking spots that say "Pastor's Parking"? (I think I like the sound of that. We need one of those at The River. I have to park way down the road on Sunday mornings.) Jesus clearly doesn't have common sense. Leaders are to be served; they are certainly not here to serve others. He didn't know the way it was supposed to be!

Or maybe Jesus did know the way it's supposed to be. Maybe he was saying that the way it is is not the way it should be. Maybe he was turning the world upside down and saying, "No, those of you in positions of power and influence ought to serve others." Maybe Jesus was saying that the way to freedom, not only others' freedom, but our own freedom, is a life spent serving other people. Others.

Jesus says in Matthew 20:28, "[I] did not come to be served, but to serve." His whole life, as the Scriptures plainly tell, was a life of throwing the "normal" way upside down. His words and his way of living tell us that a free life is a life spent serving others.

We can summarize Jesus' teaching in one word: others. Others and living for others is the way to freedom. And Jesus modeled it. Do you remember what his first miracle was? He turned water into wine at a wedding party. I mean, come on. If Jesus was like me, he'd be like, leave me alone! I'm enjoying the party, why do you want me to do anything? And especially do something about wine that's gone. But Jesus knew, and came to teach us, that life is about serving others. So he served the bride and the groom and everyone at the party. He turned water into wine not just because he could, but because he wanted to bless others.

Others. Serving others by making wine. Serving others by seeing their need and walking with them in their need and doing something about it. That's pretty cool. Not making wine—but seeing people's need and doing something about it. Serving others.

Jesus served a woman at a well in John, chapter 4. This woman had had five husbands and was currently living with someone who wasn't her husband. In that day and age it was taboo. She was a social reject. She was an outsider. She had come to the well to get water at the hottest part of the day because that was the only time of day when the other women would not be there. The other women in her community would have scorned and ridiculed her, picked on her, made fun of her. She had decided to live life alone because that was better than living a life of abuse.

So she went alone to the well and there was Jesus. And he served her by asking her to serve him.

Serving this particular woman the way he does here shows that Jesus is completely aware of the impact that his words and actions will have on her. He's a Jewish male, and most Jewish men would have had nothing to do with a Samaritan woman. He's a rabbi, a Jewish religious teacher, and a rabbi would have had nothing to do with women who had issues involving multiple husbands. Jesus knew that if he just started talking to her, his impact on her would be too great. She'd run away. She'd hear nothing of the freedom of Jesus. So he simply sits down and says, "Can you get me some water?" When we serve others, it's really important to be aware of how we come across to them.

In this dialogue of living for others, let me ask you a question. Do you know someone who just doesn't know that they're messing up the room when they walk in? You're having a great discussion and they enter in and take over, and the discussion dies. They're loud, mildly obnoxious, they bump you, and they're not even aware that they're in your personal space. And you're thinking, I wish you would leave. Or maybe if you were feeling gracious you might be thinking, I wish you were aware of your impact on others—most likely no one has ever told you about your impact. How many of you know someone who is clueless about the negative ways he or she affects others? Maybe you see that person every morning when you look in the mirror! Others. If life is to be lived for others, we must be aware of our impact.

Jesus taught us to first remove the plank from our own eye before we even consider the speck in our brother's or sister's eye. He knows that we have a tendency to be unaware of our own stuff, the great big board we have in our own eye—the board that we use to smack people around when they've just got just a little speck in their eye. The way Jesus served the woman at the well tells us he was overtly aware of his impact. Jesus came to set folks free. If he had been clueless about how the woman would react, or careless in his approach to her, there would have been no freedom for that woman. If we are such an annoyance that folks run from us, there will be no freedom for others.

Praise God, Jesus loves us even though we might annoy people from time to time. He simply wants us to be mindful and to work on not being annoying. We can begin by asking the people closest to us, "How do I come across to people?"

John, chapter 6, tells about when Jesus fed five thousand men plus many more women and children by multiplying five loaves of bread and two fish. He didn't have to do this. I mean, he was God. He could have said, "People, leave me alone. I'm busy, I'm hot, I'm tired. I need a rest. You go worry about your own food." But Jesus said, "No, I'm going to meet your need," because Jesus knew he was sent to live a life for others. Others.

Mark, chapter 1, tells that after a long stretch of ministry and praying for people and healing people late into the night, Jesus got up early the next morning. He went off to a place where he could be alone and pray. He knew that to live a life for others he had to be intimate with the Father first. He knew he would be no good to others if he didn't spend time in prayer and worship. He knew he would not be able to live for others unless he withdrew from them to meet with the Father, so that he could be aware of his impact, so he could commune with God, hear the voice of the Father. Then he could live for others. Others. Others are who it's about.

How did Jesus interact with sick people? He healed every tenth one of them, right? "You annoy me, you annoy me..." No, he healed all of them. Whenever Jesus saw a need, he met it. And he fed it. And he said, "This is good. I'm going to take care of you because I live to serve others."

I did some research on the rich, indulgent, self-serving folks of this world (a group to which most Americans belong). My research told me that people who have sold out to the narcissistic life, who have an attitude of "it's all about me," these people have the highest rates of suicide and depression. People who've intentionally said, "Screw everyone else. Life is about me and my happiness." A self serving life is not the way to freedom. It's the way to death. Others.

To live for others is a life of freedom. I'm thinking of people from my church who went to Uganda to serve the people there in many ways. These crazy people spend thousands of dollars of their own money and go live in a sweltering hut for a long time, eat food that's unfamiliar, hang out in dirty environments, and are happy. Deep down happy. I'm thinking of those who have helped with Stepping Out ministries, who just come out once in a while and serve hot dogs to the homeless. There's something good about that.

I'm thinking of those wonderful people who minister to families by watching their children and pouring Christ into them each Sunday so mom and dad can worship freely in the sanctuary. You know it would be easier for those nursery workers to come and sit in the worship service and relax. But instead they're serving others. And they're happy. I'm thinking of people who open their homes and invite people in to have community and Bible study. Those people are just happy—even though regularly hosting a group takes a lot of work.

The way to freedom is a life lived for others.

So here's the apostle Paul's word for you, taking up the teaching of

Jesus, from Philippians 2:3: "Do nothing out of selfish ambition or vain conceit. Rather, in humility value others above yourselves." Wow. That's easier said than done isn't it? Consider others as better than yourself. If you want freedom, live for others. If you want deep-seated joy, live for others.

Our homework is to forget about ourselves and live for someone else. Amen.

Prayer

We say thank you, thank you, Lord. Thank you for knowing us, thank you for numbering the hairs on our heads, thank you for loving us more than the birds of the air. Lord, you know us and you care for us, and we need to be known by you and we need to be cared for by you. So come Holy Spirit, minister in this place in ways only you can.

Go Deeper

→ Who are the "others" in your life that God is calling you to bless?
→ How you going to bless them?

Chapter 17
Confession

In Leviticus 26, verses 40 and 42, the Word of the Lord says: "If they will confess their sins...I will remember my covenant with Jacob and my covenant with Isaac and my covenant with Abraham."

"If they confess their sins..."

Israel's King David, after having committed adultery and murder, says: "I confess my iniquity; I am troubled by my sin" (Psalm 38:18).

The apostle John writes: "If we confess our sins, he is faithful and just and will forgive us our sins and purify us from all unrighteousness" (1 John 1:9).

So last Wednesday I did a good thing as a preacher. I listened to my own teaching of the Sunday before and took my own advice. I spent the day away, in solitude. I drove south to the monastery in Three Rivers, as I've done in the past, and hung out with the monks.

I noticed that they were gregarious. At 9:30 a.m. they were chatting over tea—very unusual for the monks. I ignored their gregariousness because I knew that I needed to be alone. I sat down and I said, "Hello, Abba, it's good to be back at St. Gregory's Abbey. I've missed being here with you. How would you have me spend the day?"

Within thirty seconds of having sat down, this is what I heard the Lord say to me: "Let's clear the table. I will hear your confession, my son."

No "Hello." No "Nice to see you."

"It's time to clear the table. I will hear your confession, my son."

There were thirteen things that I had to clear the table of, and get right before the Lord. I could boil them all down basically to this: in thirteen different ways, I had chosen a life of indulgence and self serving.

I came back home and had to apologize to the congregation I serve. Whether they knew it or not, they needed more from me than for me to live a life of indulgence and a lack of discipline.

Paul the apostle says in 2 Corinthians 7:10: "Godly sorrow brings repentance." I think we need to feel godly sorrow, remorse, for the way we go about life.

It's a sweeping statement that I'm making. I'm saying we all need to walk into some godly sorrow and clear the table. The Word says "godly sorrow brings repentance that leads to salvation." Repentance, as we've heard a hundred times, is changing direction. And while this is beautiful, the next part of 2 Corinthians 7:10 is key, because if you don't go on to the next few words of the verse, you could go away heavy.

"Godly sorrow brings repentance that leads to salvation *and leaves no regret...*" (emphasis added).

A lot of times our parents, our neighbors, our coaches, our friends—when we sin against them, they bring shame and condemnation, right? And you know what that sounds like: "You're a loser." "You shouldn't..." "What were you thinking?" "How can you do that?"

Shame and condemnation are not what godly repentance results in. Godly sorrow brings repentance that leads to salvation and leaves no regret. Another translation says, "Godly repentance brings remorse that leads to life." When the Lord says it's time to clear the table—"I will hear your confession"—he is inviting you and inviting me to life. See, when we don't walk into confession—"I'm sorry Lord, I've done this and this and this"—we walk in shame. But when we say, "Lord, I have done these things," the Lord says, "Thank you. Now you can have some life."

Now comes your part. Right now. It's confession time. In the book of Ezekiel, chapter 36, verse 25, the Lord, again calling people to repentance, says, "I will sprinkle clean water on you and you will be clean. I will cleanse you from all your impurities and from all your idols."

The Bible says, in James 5:16 (NRSV), "Confess your sins to one another...that you may be healed." Maybe you need to go and confess your sins to a leader in your congregation and have them pray the blessings of the forgiveness of the Lord.

Who have you hurt? Some of you have just been idiots to others. (That's a variation of "If you have a pulse, you have issues.") I know you have been an idiot from time to time. I know this because I have been, too. You have a pulse, so I know you have issues. Write a note and send it to the person you have hurt or offended. Right now. Confess to them that you have issues and that you're sorry for how you have hurt them. It's a good move for you to apologize. Do it. Right now.

Just get on your knees or lay down before the Lord and say, "I'm sorry, Lord." You don't need to ask the Lord for forgiveness, because he's already forgiven, but you do need to acknowledge in your heart that you have sinned against the Lord. Just get before the Lord and say, "I'm sorry; I confess my sins." I confess my indulgence...my sloth...my gluttony... my whatever. Confess. Right now.

Finally, thank the Lord for forgiving your sins and cleansing you of unrighteousness.

Stand with your hands raised, or sit, or kneel, or lay face down on the ground. It doesn't matter. With your voice, loudly praise the Lord for his forgiveness. Do it. Right now.

It's time for confession. Time to clear the table.

Prayer

Lord, we often don't understand, and we often lack faith, and we often ask too small. But as children of the King, Lord, we want to ask big. So right now we pray that your healing would come. We declare your kingdom come. Lord, we need your kingdom to come and bring healing to our souls and our spirits and our emotions. So we declare healing of the spirit and the soul and the emotions. Lord, I need healing of my spirit and soul and emotions.

Lord, you are good and we love you. Lord, we believe you're here today. By faith we declare it. So, Lord, do with us today what you want. We pray this in the name of Jesus. Amen.

Go Deeper

→ It's time to clear the table. What do you have to confess?

→ Who do you need to apologize to? Do it.

Chapter 18
Freedom

In addition to working at a local church, I work for the Reformed Church in America, a small denomination that has a passion for planting new churches. I help train other church planters and cast the vision for starting churches. So about once a month I call the RCA's travel agent, Missy, and say, "Missy, I need airline tickets for these dates, can you hook me up?" And she does. It's wonderful!

Recently I called and said, "Missy, I've got to go to our General Synod meeting." General Synod is the annual conference of the Reformed Church; it gathers about five hundred church leaders from all over the U.S. and Canada. I was going to present four different times on two topics: "Why We Should Plant Churches" and "Maybe You're a Church Planter."

So Missy made the arrangements and I flew out to Sioux Falls, South Dakota, on a Wednesday. I landed, got my rental car, and started driving from Sioux Falls, through Minnesota, and on over to northwest Iowa, where General Synod was being held. I called my supervisor to ask him where we should meet the next day to plan things. He said, "Tell me you're not in Iowa."

Oh crap! I was in Iowa the wrong week! I called Missy back. "Missy, I gotta get back to Kalamazoo, Michigan, and I need to get back here next week. Can you help?"

The wrong week! Can you believe it? Who does that happen to? I'm anal retentive. That does not happen to me. I cross the t's and dot the i's. Oh my goodness. Can you believe that?

Freedom. You know, I'm going to give you freedom to laugh at me about that. I'm going to give you freedom to make fun of me and cajole me and rib me good naturedly, because it's a funny thing.

Freedom is a wonderful thing, don't you agree? It's awesome.

We see how wonderful freedom is by looking at its absence in world history. Look at the darkest spot on American history. Slavery. How awful. I'm sure you've read or heard the stories in your history classes of the lack of freedom that slaves endured and the terrible things white people did to them because they were not people with freedom, they were possessions to be owned.

Family members were separated, never to see each other again, ever. Because some white dude thought it would be more profitable to separate them and sell them. The lack of freedom is awful. Can you imagine your family standing up on the trading block, and someone saying, "You go that way, you go this way, and the kids will go another way." Never to see each other again. The absence of freedom is horrific.

Colonial Ireland was ruled by the English. Wealthy Protestant Englishmen would come to the farms of poor Irish Catholic people and say, "You no longer own this land and I do; it's mine. Leave." Families with boatloads of kids suddenly had no place to live, no place where they could provide for themselves. They'd go live in the hill country, and they would starve and die and bury their children in ditches. The absence of freedom is horrific.

Think of apartheid in South Africa, where a small minority of whites ruled the large black majority very cruelly and unjustly. The lack of freedom is horrific.

Think about you and me. I'm thinking of addictions, substance abuse, anger issues, lust issues. Freedom is wonderful and the lack of it is awful. I'm thinking of people who are stuck in broken marriages or stuck in poverty. People who are stuck in loneliness, without companionship. The lack of freedom is awful.

The Bible has a few things to say about freedom. In Scripture the word *free* in different forms is used over eighty-four times. Psalm 146:7 says, "[God] upholds the cause of the oppressed and gives food to the hungry. The Lord sets prisoners free." Amen. Have you ever been a prisoner to something—to anger, to lust, to brokenness? Hear the word of the Lord. God brings freedom for the oppressed and sets prisoners free.

Romans 6:18 says, "You have been set free from sin and have become slaves to righteousness." Amen. Over in chapter 8, same book, verse 21, it says, "The creation itself will be liberated from its bondage to decay and brought into the glorious freedom of the children of God."

Or how about 2 Corinthians 3:17: "Now the Lord is the Spirit, and where the Spirit of the Lord is, there is freedom." Freedom.

The first chapter of the book of Revelation, verse 5 (NRSV), says, "To him [Jesus] who loves us and freed us from our sins by his blood...be glory and dominion for ever and ever." Freedom is a wonderful thing. And its absence is horrific.

Do you know what it is to not be free? Not long ago, my grandfather was buried in Arlington National Cemetery. My father is a retired air force man, and we stayed on the military base and drove into the cemetery through a gate where a soldier was standing guard. We went through the gate five times with my father driving. He looks like a military man, straight and tight, starched shirts.

I had to take my brother to the airport, and as I tried to drive through the same gate we had come in through before, the guard dude says, "I can't let you in here."

"What are you talking about?"

"I'm sorry, sir, this gate is not for reentry." The man had a gun.

"How can you tell me that? I've already been through here five times in another vehicle."

"I'm sorry, sir, this gate is not for reentry."

"This is silly, your inconsistency is just silly. What are you thinking!"

"I'm sorry, sir, I can't let you through this gate."

You know what he got from me? I said, "This is stupid, Rent-a-cop." I turned around, rolled up the window, and felt like I was going to puke. I was so mad. I mean I wasn't just a little angry, I was mad! Rage. My body got tight, my language got embarrassing, and I began to hit the steering wheel. Who the bleep does this guy think he is? What is he thinking?

I thought the guy was an idiot. He wasn't; he was just doing his job. I was the idiot. But I thought about this guy for two days. How could he not let me in when he let us in earlier? What is he thinking? Is it because I look like I do that he's not letting me in? Who does he think he is? For two days I stewed over this.

The lack of freedom is deadly. Do you know what I'm talking about? You see, when we walk in bondage, it does bad things to our body. I was not free.

The Bible has a lot to say about freedom. In fact the business of Jesus is your freedom.

So what does freedom look like? We've looked at the absence of freedom, but what about the presence of freedom?

It might look something like this. You find yourself in Iowa, having spent a thousand plus dollars flying out to a meeting during the wrong week. The lack-of-freedom response would be, "I'm such an idiot!" "How could I have done this?" "What a moron." "I'm stupid." "I'm an idiot." Or maybe, "It's gotta be their fault."

The presence-of-freedom response looks like this: "Wow, that was stupid, but this is a funny story. I can't wait to tell people so we can all laugh." Freedom is good. I'm going to assume that you like freedom. I liked my response when I just said, "Oh well, silly me."

I didn't like my response to the military guy, when I wasn't free. I was rude, condescending, and downright mean. The absence of freedom is horrific.

So what made the difference? Where does freedom come from? Let's do some addition: 14:6 plus 8:32 equals freedom. John 14:6 (NRSV)— Jesus says "I am the way, and the truth, and the life"...the way, the truth, *and life*. John 8:32—Jesus says, "You will know the truth, and the truth will set you free." Add these passages together: Jesus is the truth, and the truth will set you free.

The way to freedom is Jesus. I've known Jesus for most of my life, and yet not long ago I found myself in bondage and anger. Then the following week, the week I flew to Iowa, I found myself in freedom. What's the difference? Did I have Jesus in Iowa, but not in Arlington? No, I had him in both places. The difference was in how close I was to him.

The key to freedom is intimacy with Jesus. The truth will set you free. Jesus is truth and life. What I'm getting at is that it's not enough to call on Jesus one time and say, "Now I'll live in freedom for the rest of my life." In order to walk in freedom when life throws punches at us, we need to be with Jesus on a regular, daily basis.

If you want to be free, get with Jesus. The source of our freedom is Jesus. Close proximity.

How does that happen? The Bible tells us something about that. Going back to the beginning, in the Old Testament, the book of Exodus, chapter 3, verse 7, we read that God's people were in bondage. And the Lord said, "I have indeed seen the misery of my people in Egypt. I have heard them crying out." We read further on, in the book of Judges, chapter 6, that when the Israelites cried to the Lord in their misery he sent a deliverer and they were free.

Moving ahead to 1 Samuel, Hannah wanted a kid. She didn't have any kids. She cried out to the Lord. And the Lord heard her prayer. In the book of Psalms, chapter 72, verse 12, it says, "For he will deliver the needy who cry out."

The key to our freedom is Jesus. Cry out to the Lord. If you are grumpy and tired, don't yell at your husband or your wife, yell to the Lord. If you're tired of being depressed, cry out to the Lord. As humans our nature is to get so focused right here. Woe is me, woe is this, woe is that. Well, stop it. Throw whatever it is to the Lord and say, "Lord, I'm tired of it. You take it."

Cry out and freedom will follow. Then once you've cried out, work it out. Cry out then work it out. The apostle Paul says in the book of Philippians, chapter 2, verse 12, "[W]ork out your salvation." He doesn't say work for your salvation. Jesus already gave it to us. He says to work it out. So there's an element here of us getting busy. We can't just come to church and say, "Oh, Jesus loves me." We have to get off our butts and work out the freedom that God has given us.

If you're tired of being an alcoholic, get off your butt and go to AA. If you're tired of depression, get up, go see a therapist, get on some drugs, and get around some godly people who will walk with you. Work it out. Get up and do something about it. How many of you are tired of your physical state? Maybe you're tired of being a smoker. Well, quit. Work it out. Do whatever you have to do to work it out. How many of you are tired, not in as good a shape as you were when you were younger? You think, "Man, I used to be fit, I was thin!" Well, work it out. Get up and do something. Moping and crying and complaining won't get us anywhere. Get up and work it out. Cry out and work it out, and the freedom will find you and you will be free.

As followers of Christ, we are the children of Abba. And the Father loves us. And God is good to us. But we also need to know that our walk requires us to do something. Not that we're earning salvation, but we've got to walk into the gift that's been given to us. It's time to walk into freedom by shaking off whatever we need to shake off and moving in the direction the Lord has for us. Let's move!

Prayer

Come, Holy Spirit. Bring your joy, Lord, for many of us need joy. Lord, we ask for the joy of Jesus, the abundant life that you promise. Lord, we pray against the work of the enemy who wants to steal, kill, and destroy and bring despair, discouragement, and depression. Lord, we pray against the lies of the father of lies and the accusations of the accuser of the brethren, and we say no in the name of Jesus, and we say yes to the joy of Christ.

Go Deeper

→ How close and regular are you in your walk with Jesus?

→ What does it look like for you to walk with Jesus?

→ What do you need to "work out"?

Chapter 19
Praise

Are you on Facebook? Have you found yourself highly annoyed with Facebook? Facebook has been a source of annoyance for me for years. Have you thought, "I don't care about your farm!"? I don't care that you found a lonely llama, and now it has a pack of llamas to hang out with. I just don't care.

And those little reminders: You've got such-and-such a meeting to go to, this or that event. I don't care. It's so-and-so's birthday. Who cares? You haven't thought of them in years. But, ding! "It's so-and-so's birthday. Remind her that it's her birthday. Say Happy Birthday." I don't care! Or at least I didn't until my birthday.

Before my birthday, whenever I would get the little reminder that it was the birthday of George—my friend I haven't seen in six years who lives in Tennessee—my thought was, "If I send him a happy birthday note it is going to come across as disingenuous, contrived, forced, 'cause he's going to say, 'Link wasn't thinking of me. He just has Facebook and got a reminder.'"

But when I turned thirty-nine years old, my outlook on Facebook changed. At the time I had 224 friends and a little over half of them sent me birthday wishes. And do you know what I did *not* think? "That's forced; that's contrived; that's disingenuous." No, I didn't think that at all. Rather, I was, quite simply, blessed.

Some of the birthday wishes were short: "Happy birthday." I imagine that many of the people wishing me happy birthday were simply reminded by Facebook and without it they would not have thought of me at all. But it didn't bother me. I really appreciated those two words: happy birthday. Other folks, a little more verbose, sent two paragraphs. One wrote, "Link, I'm so glad you were born." That blessed me! What if Facebook hadn't sent the message: ding! "It's Rob Link's birthday"? My birthday would have been less sweet. Facebook is my friend. Although I still don't care about your lost llama and your farm.

All I'm doing is reminding you that throughout biblical history and the history of the Christian church, a powerful move of the Lord has rarely been ushered in by great teaching. Whenever the Lord showed up in force and people were set free, healed in their spirits and bodies in big numbers, whenever people found freedom and victory, whenever God swept through a nation, and that nation went from worshiping false gods to worshiping the one true God—those moves of God hardly ever came on the heels of great preaching.

You might think this is mildly problematic for me, being a preacher by trade. But the reality is that great preaching can actually get in the way of a move of the Lord. We've seen this happen throughout American church history, beginning in the Enlightenment in the seventeenth century. That's when people, including Christians, began to value knowledge above almost everything. We became a bunch of Christian bobbleheads. We have huge heads stuffed with knowledge of the Bible, but we don't know how to put it into practice. We've become pew potatoes, so well-fed on the word of God that we can't get up!

What the kingdom needs is less good teaching and more "good doing"—doing what we've already been taught. The kingdom needs more of God's people doing what the teaching says. Here's what I want to focus on right now, our commission from Hebrews 13:15: "Therefore, let us continually offer to God a sacrifice of praise."

The point of walking with God is to praise the Lord. The point of gathering for worship isn't simply to get good teaching, so that we can speculate about what the teaching means and file it away in our catalogue of knowledge. We gather to hear the word of God so that we might do the word of God.

Throughout biblical history, powerful moves of the Lord have always been ushered in not by good teaching but by the prayer and praise of God's people. In 2 Chronicles 7:14, God says to Israel, "If my people, who are called by my name, will humble themselves and pray and seek my face and turn from their wicked ways, then I will hear from heaven and will forgive their sin and will heal their land." So if you don't want an encounter with the Lord, don't pray and don't offer praise. But if you really want an encounter with the King of kings and Lord of lords, if you want Sunday to be a lot more than just something you check off your to-do list—if you want to be able to say, "I encountered God!"—

the key is to offer God a sacrifice, a sacrifice of praise.

Our commission, what we are called to do as members of the kingdom of God, as Hebrews 13 makes clear, is to offer praise. You might be saying to yourself, You know what? I wouldn't be praising God and singing songs to glorify God without the pastor reminding me to. It seems disingenuous. It seems contrived. It seems kind of forced.

Remember how I said that my birthday was a good day because Facebook reminded people who wouldn't have thought of it otherwise to simply honor me? If you are like my pre-thirty-ninth-birthday self, you may be thinking, I can't just worship; the pastor's just telling me to worship. It feels forced and contrived. I don't feel like worshiping today.

Here's what I want to tell you: Get over it! The Lord will be blessed whenever you offer a sacrifice of praise. You have an opportunity right now to bless the Lord by honoring him, by offering him a sacrifice of praise. You might need to simply say something like "Happy birthday." That's fine! Two words are all you need to give the Lord, and he'll love it. Some of you, though, have got a couple of paragraphs in you, and you might need to offer that to the Lord. Just offer your sacrifice of praise.

When we offer praise (I'm using worship and praise interchangeably here), about a million things happen. I want to point out two of those things. Number one, we're reminded in worship that it (life, etc.) is really about God, not about us. Worship puts things in the right perspective. When we look to God, it keeps us from focusing on things like "I had a bad day," "They don't like me," " I don't have enough money," "I got no friends." Me, me, me; woe is me; life stinks. Well, when you take your eyes off your own belly button and raise them to the King of kings and Lord of lords, you're saying, "It's about you, Lord; it's not about me." Your perspective changes.

Secondly, when we worship, the One who it's really about turns it around and says, "Because I am yours, it is about you; and I'm going to pick you up out of the junk that you're in." You'll be picked up out of the junk you're in by offering God praise. Worship is not about you; it's about him. And when we worship and see that it's about him, we get a sense that all will be well.

Embracing worship was a bit of a struggle for me. Back in college, when I attended the weekly Fellowship of Christian Athletes meetings I would go late to skip the worship. I had never seen any men worshiping with gusto when I was younger (except the pastor, but he wore a bathrobe—he called it an "alb"—to church, so I certainly didn't want to be like him). I wrongly thought worship was women's work. Holy cow! I couldn't have been more wrong. It is no exaggeration to say that today I am most free when I'm worshiping.

In the United States the music industry is a $12.9 billion business. I believe this is in large part because all humans (not just women) were made to worship or sing unto something. The huge popularity of song in our culture, and in all the world's cultures, stems from our longing to sing to something. When folks don't have Jesus they try to meet this innate need to worship by singing along with Springsteen, U2, Lady Gaga, or whoever. Because so many people are without Christ, many unknowingly worship whatever and whoever is popular at the moment. Yet make no mistake, singing along with pop songs is no substitute for worshiping the King of kings. Before we were made to sing along with a CD, we were made to sing unto the Lord.

Our commission is to continually offer a sacrifice of praise. So here's a word of instruction to help you get at your commission. When you offer your sacrifice of praise, be sure to sit on your hands and don't forget to scowl!

Seriously though, it's good to be free in worship before the Lord. So be free as you worship and offer your sacrifice of praise. Your freedom might mean just sittin' and chillin'. Your freedom might mean raising your hand. Your freedom might mean bouncing with the music. Your freedom might mean getting on your knees before the Lord. Your freedom is your freedom. Offer your sacrifice of praise.

King David, as it says in the book of 1 Kings, was so happy in the Lord that he stripped down to his skivvies and just danced before the Lord. I'm sure not suggesting that we take our clothes off in worship like David, but from his example we learn that it's good to be free in worship before the Lord.

Be free in worship and offer your sacrifice of praise. Just be sure to keep your clothes on.

Prayer

Lord, remind us of all the ways you have blessed us, as individuals, as the body of Christ, as a nation. Lord, you have blessed us, and we say thank you. We ask that your presence would bring the joy and the peace that come only from being in your company. Come, Holy Spirit, come. Lord, we invite your spirit to come and bring with it the hope of a future. Come, Holy Spirit; we need you.

We invite your spirit, Lord, to move within us, to flow through us and blow away any religious practices that lead us to sit back and speculate and watch. We want an encounter with the King of kings and Lord of lords. Lord, transform us and set us free. We ask that all that would distract us would be removed. We ask that the kingdom of darkness would flee. Come, Holy Spirit. In the name of Jesus. Amen!

Go Deeper

→ Turn on your iPod, crank up the CD, and worship!

Additional Reading

Abba's Child: The Cry of the Heart for Intimate Belonging, by Brennan Manning ((NavPress, 2002)

The Complete Collection of Calvin and Hobbes, by Bill Watterson (Andrews McMeel Publishing, 2005)

Mindset: The New Psychology of Success, by Carol Dweck (Ballantine Books, 2008)

The Ragamuffin Gospel, by Brennan Manning (Multnomah Publishers, Inc., 2000)

Remembering a Forgotten Grace: Thoughts on Shame, Beauty, Romance and Radiance, by Rod Tucker (Hope Publishing House, 2008)

Two Hours to Freedom: A Simple and Effective Model for Healing and Deliverance, by Charles Kraft (Chosen, 2010)

Waking the Dead: The Glory of a Heart Fully Alive, by John Eldredge (Thomas Nelson, Inc., 2005)

Wild at Heart: Discovering the Secret of a Man's Soul, by John Eldredge (Thomas Nelson, Inc., 2002)